Elizabeth Gundrey was well k...
Britain's first consumer magazine...
long before she turned her keen ...
value for money to the subject o...
books, *Staying Off the Beaten Tr*...
Wales has been by far the most p......
the bestseller in its field. For the *Scotland* edition,
she has joined forces with Nancy Webber, one of
the editors of *England and Wales* in its early years.

VOUCHERS WORTH £18
(by courtesy of the houses concerned)

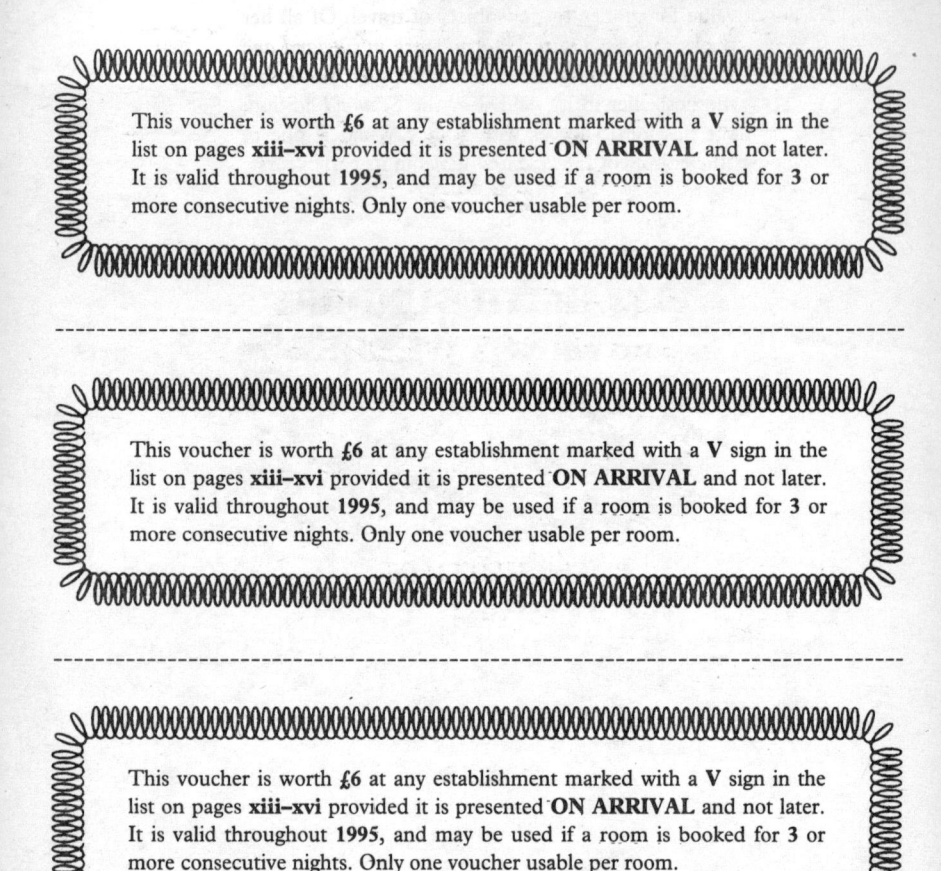

This voucher is worth **£6** at any establishment marked with a **V** sign in the list on pages **xiii–xvi** provided it is presented **ON ARRIVAL** and not later. It is valid throughout **1995**, and may be used if a room is booked for **3** or more consecutive nights. Only one voucher usable per room.

This voucher is worth **£6** at any establishment marked with a **V** sign in the list on pages **xiii–xvi** provided it is presented **ON ARRIVAL** and not later. It is valid throughout **1995**, and may be used if a room is booked for **3** or more consecutive nights. Only one voucher usable per room.

This voucher is worth **£6** at any establishment marked with a **V** sign in the list on pages **xiii–xvi** provided it is presented **ON ARRIVAL** and not later. It is valid throughout **1995**, and may be used if a room is booked for **3** or more consecutive nights. Only one voucher usable per room.

STAYING OFF THE BEATEN TRACK
IN SCOTLAND
1995

ELIZABETH GUNDREY
and NANCY WEBBER

*A personal selection of moderately priced
guest-houses, small hotels, farms and country houses*

**1st EDITION
1995**

ARROW

Published by Arrow Books Limited in 1994

1 3 5 7 9 10 8 6 4 2

First published in Great Britain 1994

Copyright © 1994 by Elizabeth Gundrey

Elizabeth Gundrey has asserted her right to be identified as the author of this work in accordance with the Copyright, Designs and Patents Act, 1988

This book is sold subject to the condition that it shall not, by way of trade or otherwise, be lent, resold, hired out, or otherwise circulated without the publisher's prior consent in any form of binding or cover other than that in which it is published and without a similar condition including this condition being imposed on the subsequent purchaser

Arrow Books Limited
20 Vauxhall Bridge Road, London, SW1V 2SA

Random House Australia (Pty) Limited
20 Alfred Street, Milsons Point, Sydney,
New South Wales 2061, Australia

Random House New Zealand Limited
18 Poland Road, Glenfield,
Auckland 10, New Zealand

Random House South Africa (Pty) Limited
PO Box 337, Bergvlei, South Africa

Random House UK Limited Reg. No. 954009

Printed and bound in Great Britain by
The Guernsey Press Co. Limited, Guernsey, C.I.

Cover pictures: **Aultmore House,** Highland (front, bottom)
Tigh na Mara, Highland (front, top; back)

A CIP catalogue record for this book is available from the British Library

ISBN 0-09-935821 2

The author and publishers would like to thank all those owners who allowed us to use their drawings. Additional line drawings by Rhona Garvin.

Although every care has been taken to ensure that all the information in this book is correct and up to date, neither the author nor the publishers can accept responsibility for details which may have changed since the book went to press.

Acknowledgments

We would like to thank the Scottish Tourist Board and the following regional tourist boards for help: East Lothian Tourist Board, Grampian, Highland and Aberdeen Tourist Board, Perthshire Tourist Board and Scottish Borders Tourist Board. Also InterCity (London) and Motorail (Scotland); and Grants of Aviemore (hire cars).

We also acknowledge with much appreciation the assistance of the rest of the SOTBT team (Walter Gundrey, Jennifer Christie and Bob Vickers) as well as all the proprietors of houses.

Elizabeth Gundrey
and Nancy Webber

DATES IN SCOTTISH HISTORY

1040	Macbeth succeeds Duncan
1057	Macbeth succeeded by Duncan's son Malcolm
1296	William Wallace defeats English at Stirling Bridge
1298	Wallace defeated by Edward I at Falkirk
1305	Wallace executed in London
1314	Robert Bruce defeats Edward II at Bannockburn
1503	James IV marries Margaret Tudor, daughter of Henry VII
1513	James killed at Flodden; accession of James V at 17 months old
1542	Mary Queen of Scots succeeds to throne at one week old
1557	Protestant nobles draw up 'First Covenant' against Rome
1558	Mary marries Francis, Dauphin of France
1560	First General Assembly of the Church of Scotland
1561	Francis dies; Mary returns to Scotland
1565	Mary marries Lord Darnley, who also has a claim to the English throne through his grandmother Margaret Tudor
1567	Darnley murdered; Mary marries James Hepburn, Earl of Bothwell. Mary forced to abdicate in favour of James VI
1568	Mary flees to England
1581	'Negative Confession' against Rome, the 'Second Covenant', signed by James
1587	Execution of Mary Queen of Scots in England
1592	Presbyterianism established by Act of Parliament
1603	Elizabeth of England dies; James succeeds to English throne
1625	James VI and I dies
1633	Charles I crowned in Scotland
1637	Introduction of 'Laud's Liturgy'
1638	'National Covenant' against Rome and recent innovations signed. General Assembly restores presbyterianism
1643	'Solemn League and Covenant' signed by English Parliament and Scottish Covenanters
1649	Execution of Charles I in England
1660	Restoration of Charles II
1661	Restoration of episcopacy
1685	Accession of James VII and II
1688	'Glorious Revolution'; accession of William III and Mary
1689	Rising in support of deposed James VII; victory at Killiecrankie; defeat at Dunkeld
1692	Massacre of Glencoe
1707	Union of Parliaments
1715	Rising in support of James VIII and III, the 'Old Pretender'; defeat at Sheriffmuir
1745	Rising in support of Prince Charles Edward Stuart, the 'Young Pretender'; victory at Prestonpans
1746	Defeat at Culloden

CONTENTS

Maps of Scotland	viii
You and the law	xii
Regional list of houses and hotels	xiii
Introduction	xvii
Reader participation	xix
How to have a good time	xxi
How to get to Scotland	xxiii
Books to read	xxiv
The Scottish Wildlife Trust	xxv
Highland Games in 1995	xxvii
Explanation of code letters	xxviii
Alphabetical directory of houses and hotels	1
Order for *England and Wales* edition	132

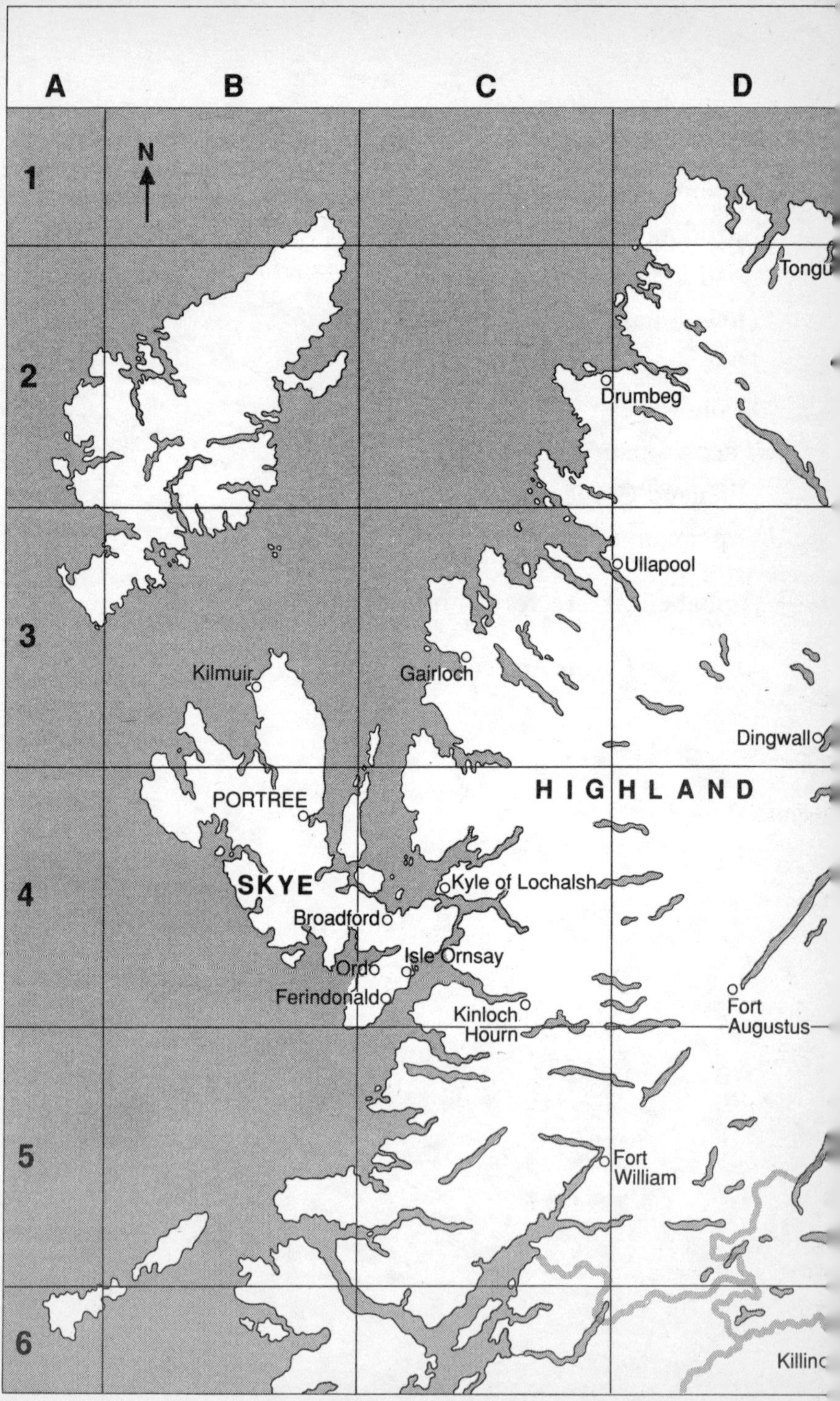
A
B
C
D
1
2
3
4
5
6
N
Tongu
Drumbeg
Ullapool
Kilmuir
Gairloch
Dingwall
HIGHLAND
PORTREE
SKYE
Kyle of Lochalsh
Broadford
Isle Ornsay
Ord
Ferindonald
Kinloch
Hourn
Fort
Augustus
Fort
William
Killinc

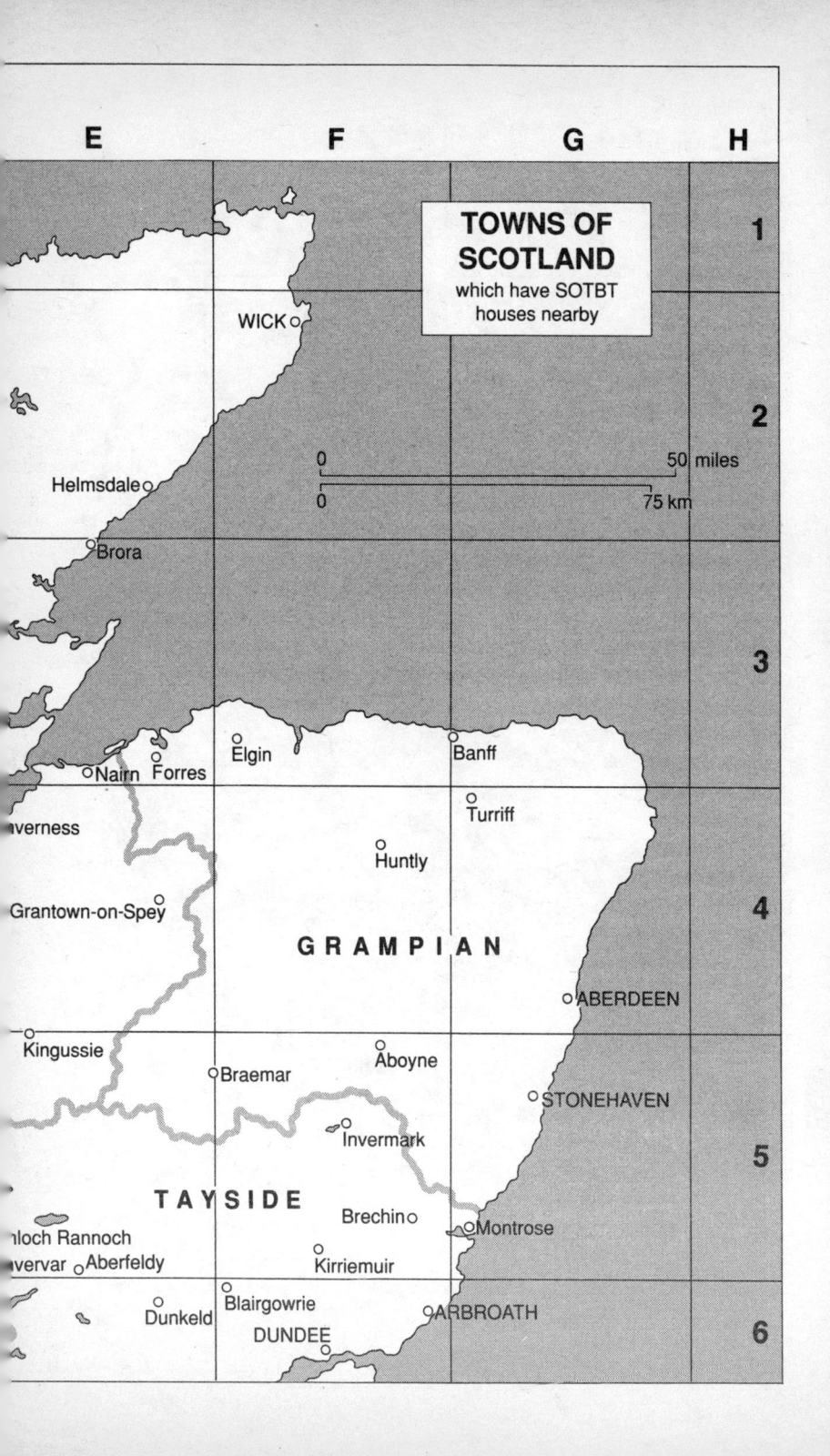

TOWNS OF SCOTLAND
which have SOTBT houses nearby

	E	F	G	H
1		WICK		
2	Helmsdale			
3	Brora			
4	Nairn, Forres / Inverness / Grantown-on-Spey	Elgin / Huntly	Banff / Turriff / **GRAMPIAN**	ABERDEEN
5	Kingussie	Braemar / Aboyne / Invermark / **TAYSIDE**	Brechin / Montrose	STONEHAVEN
6	loch Rannoch / vervar, Aberfeldy	Dunkeld / Blairgowrie / DUNDEE / Kirriemuir	ARBROATH	

0 ——— 50 miles
0 ——— 75 km

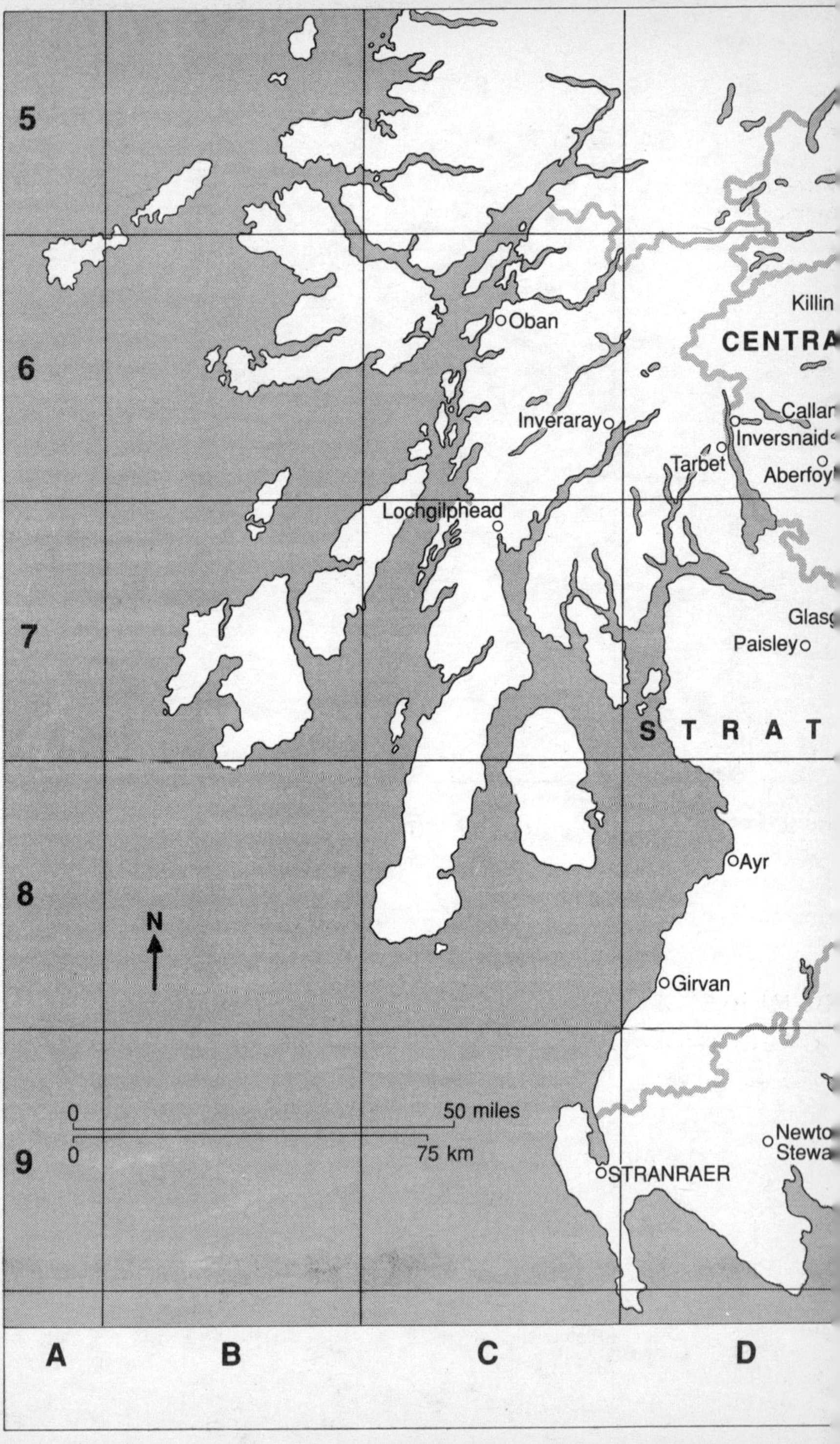

5
6
7
8
9
A
B
C
D
N
Oban
Killin
CENTRA
Inveraray
Callan
Inversnaid
Tarbet
Aberfoy
Lochgilphead
Glasg
Paisley
S T R A T
Ayr
Girvan
0
50 miles
0
75 km
Newto
Stewa
STRANRAER

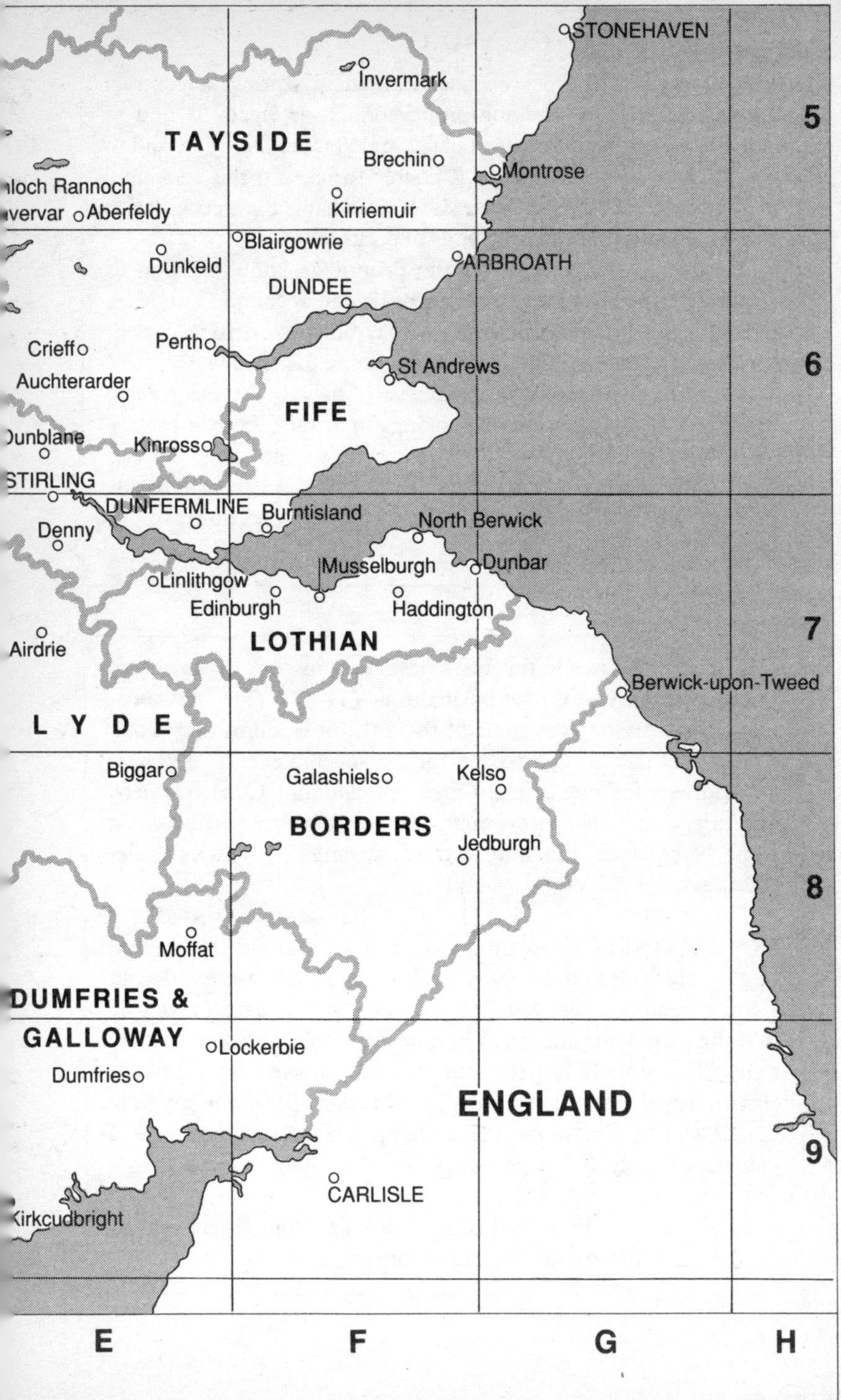

STONEHAVEN
Invermark
5
TAYSIDE
Brechin
Montrose
loch Rannoch
Kirriemuir
vervar
Aberfeldy
Blairgowrie
ARBROATH
Dunkeld
DUNDEE
Crieff
Perth
St Andrews
6
Auchterarder
FIFE
Dunblane
Kinross
STIRLING
DUNFERMLINE
Burntisland
North Berwick
Denny
Musselburgh
Dunbar
Linlithgow
Edinburgh
Haddington
7
Airdrie
LOTHIAN
Berwick-upon-Tweed
LYDE
Biggar
Galashiels
Kelso
BORDERS
Jedburgh
8
Moffat
DUMFRIES &
GALLOWAY
Lockerbie
Dumfries
ENGLAND
9
CARLISLE
Kirkcudbright
E
F
G
H

YOU AND THE LAW

Once your booking has been confirmed in writing, a contract exists between you and the proprietor. He is legally bound to provide accommodation as booked; and you are legally bound to pay for this accommodation. If unable to take up the booking – even because of sickness – you still remain liable for a cancellation charge (in addition to losing your deposit).

If you have to cancel, let the proprietor know as soon as possible; then he may be able to re-let the accommodation (in which case you would be liable to pay only a re-letting cost or forfeit your deposit). Phone if you are going to arrive late.

(**A note to American readers.** It may be an acceptable practice elsewhere to make bookings at several houses for the same date, choosing only later which one to patronise; but this way of doing things is not the British practice and you are legally liable to compensate any proprietors whom you let down in this way.)

NOTE: The houses in this book have been inspected. **At any of them you may stay for as little as £11–£20 (for bed-and-breakfast)** although at some of them the best rooms cost more. Prices may rise at high season, or for specific events (e.g. near St Andrews for the British Open and Dunhill Cup). Owners, and prices, can change overnight; so check before you book. At some places, you can dine without staying: see entries under **'Dinner'**.

COMPLAINTS: If anything was not of reasonable standard (e.g. chilly bedroom or badly cooked food) you are entitled to claim a reduction on your bill, but *only if* you have previously told the proprietor and given him or her a chance to put matters right. We regularly inspect; and also will forward complaints to proprietors. Owners are normally anxious to put right anything that is wrong. Please enclose a stamped addressed envelope if you want a reply. See page xix.

Readers' comments quoted in the book are from letters sent to us: they are not supplied via the proprietors.

REGIONAL LIST OF HOUSES & HOTELS

The hotels and houses appear in the main part of this book in alphabetical order. However, for convenience in locating them, they are grouped in the following list according to regions. On the left is the nearest town (sometimes distant), with its map reference (see pages viii–xi), followed by the house or hotel and its nearest village.

Establishments marked with a V will accept the discount vouchers from page ii. Other discounts to readers are described in the text.

Nearest town	Map ref. (see p. viii-xi)		Address	Page
BORDERS				
(Berwick-upon-Tweed, Northumberland)	G.7		Castle Rock, St Abbs	26
		V	Harelawside Farm, Grantshouse	56
		V	St Albans, Duns	105
Galashiels	F.8	V	Torwood Lodge, Melrose	120
Jedburgh	F.8		Greenhill, Hownam	55
		V	Willow Court	129
Kelso	G.8	V	Paramount, Town Yetholm	97
			Whitehill Farm, Nenthorn	127
		V	Whitehouse, St Boswells	128
CENTRAL				
Aberfoyle	D.6	V	Inversnaid Lodge, Inversnaid	64
Callander	D.6	V	Arden House	6
		V	Roslin Cottage, Lagrannoch	103
Denny	E.7	V	Lochend Farm, Carronbridge	79
		V	Topps Farm	118
Dunblane	E.6	V	The Linns, Blair Drummond	76
		V	Mackeanston House, Doune	82
Killin	D.6		Breadalbane House	21
(Linlithgow, Lothian)	E.7	V	2 Bonhard Cottages, Bo'ness	19
DUMFRIES & GALLOWAY				
Dumfries	E.9	V	Glebe House, Terregles	49
		V	Locharthur House, Beeswing	78
Kirkcudbright	E.9		The Rossan, Auchencairn	104
Lockerbie	E.9	V	Kirkside of Middlebie	70
		V	Magdalene House, Lochmaben	83
		V	Nether Boreland Farm, Boreland	89

xiii

Nearest town	Map ref. (see p. viii–xi)		Address	Page
Moffat	E.8		Corehead Farm, Annan Water	28
		V	Ericstane Farm	41
		V	Hartfell House	57
		V	Woodhead Farm	130
Newton Stewart	D.9		Auchenleck Farm, Minnigaff	10
		V	Flowerbank, Cree Bridge	45

FIFE

Burntisland	F.7		Hawkcraig House, Aberdour	58
St Andrews	F.6		Caiplie, Crail	25
			Edenside	39
			Milton Farm, Leuchars	87

GRAMPIAN

Aboyne	F.5	V	Birkwood Lodge	16
Banff	G.3	V	Academy House, Fordyce	2
		V	Montcoffer House	88
Braemar	E.5	V	Schiehallion House	107
Elgin	F.3	V	Foresters House, Newton	46
Forres	E.3	V	Blervie	18
		V	Scania	106
(Grantown-on-Spey, Highland)	E.4	V	Croughly Farm, Tomintoul	30
Huntly	F.4		Earlsfield Farm, Kennethmont	36
			Faich Hill Farm, Gartly	43
(Montrose, Tayside)	G.5		Kirkgate House, St Cyrus	69
Turriff	G.4	V	Lendrum Farm, Birkenhills	74

HIGHLAND

Brora	E.3	V	Clynelish Farm	27
Dingwall	D.3		Old Manse, Fodderty	92
Drumbeg	C.2	V	Taigh Druimbeag	111
Fort Augustus	D.4	V	Old Pier House	93
Fort William	C.5		Ardsheal Home Farm, Kentallen	7
			Invergloy House, Spean Bridge	63
		V	Old Pines, Spean Bridge	94
Gairloch	C.3		Little Lodge, North Erradale	77
		V	Old Smiddy, Laide	95
Grantown-on-Spey	E.4		Aultmore House, Nethybridge	11
		V	Avingormack, Boat of Garten	12
		V	(Croughly Farm, see Grampian)	30
		V	Dalrachney House, Carrbridge	32
			Heathbank, Boat of Garten	59
Helmsdale	E.2	V	Broomhill House	23

Nearest town	Map ref. (see p. viii-xi)		Address	Page
Inverness	E.4	V	Easter Dalziel Farm, Dalcross	37
		V	Enrick Cottage, Drumnadrochit	40
		V	Daviot Mains Farm, Daviot	33
			Torguish House, Daviot	119
		V	Wester Moniack Farm, Kirkhill	125
Kingussie	E.5	V	Alvie Manse, Alvie	4
			Braeriach, Kincraig	20
		V	Kirkbeag, Kincraig	68
		V	March House, Feshiebridge	85
		V	Osprey Hotel	96
Kinloch Hourn	C.4		Skiary	110
Kyle of Lochalsh	C.4		Craig Highland Farm, Plockton	29
Nairn	E.3	V	Brightmony Farmhouse, Auldearn	22
Tongue	D.2	V	Rhian Cottage	102
Ullapool	D.3		The Sheiling	109
			Tigh na Mara, Ardindrean	116

LOTHIAN

Dunbar	F.7	V	Hope Cottage, Stenton	61
			Tynefield	122
Edinburgh	F.7		Ashdene House	9
		V	The Galloway	47
		V	Kildonan Lodge	66
		V	9/B Scotland Street	108
Haddington	F.7		Barney Mains	14
		V	Eaglescairnie Mains, Gifford	35
Linlithgow	E.7	V	(2 Bonhard Cottages, see Central)	19
Musselburgh	F.7		53 Eskside West	42
North Berwick	F.7	V	Glebe House	48

STRATHCLYDE

Airdrie	E.7	V	Easter Glentore Farm, Greengairs	38
Ayr	D.8		Dunduff Farm, Dunure	34
		V	Low Coylton House, Coylton	81
Biggar	E.8	V	Glentewing Farm, Crawfordjohn	52
		V	Netherton Farm, Abington	91
		V	Townfoot Farm, Roberton	121
Girvan	D.8		Balkissock Lodge, Ballantrae	13
			Glendrissaig	50
Glasgow	D.7		148 Queen's Drive	101

Nearest town	Map ref. (see p. viii-xi)		Address	Page
Inveraray	C.6		Arnish Cottage, Poll Bay	8
			Portinnisherrich Farm, by Dalmally	99
		V	Thistle House, St Catherines	114
Lochgilphead	C.7	V	Kirnan, Kilmichael Glen	71
			Tibertich Farm, Kilmartin	115
Oban	C.6	V	Lerags House, Lerags	75
		V	Lochside Cottage, Fasnacloich	80
Paisley	D.7		High Belltrees Farm, Lochwinnoch	60
Tarbet	D.6	V	Tarbet House	112

TAYSIDE

Nearest town	Map ref.		Address	Page
Aberfeldy	E.5		Invervar Lodge, Invervar	65
			Tigh'n Eilean	117
Auchterarder	E.6	V	Glentower House, Glen Devon	53
			Lawhill House, Trinity Gask	73
			Nether Coul	90
Blairgowrie	F.6	V	Alyth Hotel, Alyth	5
		V	Blair View, Glenshee	17
		V	Glenmarkie Farmhouse, Glenisla	51
			Mains of Soilzarie, Bridge of Cally	84
Brechin	F.5		The House of Mark, Invermark	62
Crieff	E.6	V	Miller's Field, Dalginross	86
Dunkeld	E.6		Bheinne Mhor, Birnam	15
		V	Upper Woodinch, Dalguise	123
Kinloch Rannoch	E.5	V	Bunrannoch House	24
		V	Cuilmore Cottage	31
		V	West Tempar House	124
Kinross	E.6		Whistlebare, Milnathort	126
Kirriemuir	F.5	V	Purgavie Farm, Lintrathen	100
Montrose	G.5		(Kirkgate House, see Grampian)	69
Perth	E.6		Gloagburn Farm, Tibbermore	54
		V	Pitmurthly Farm, Redgorton	98

ISLE OF SKYE

Nearest town	Map ref.		Address	Page
Broadford	C.4		Langdale House, Waterloo	72
Ferindonald	C.4	V	Alltan	3
Isle Ornsay	C.4		Tawny Croft	113
Kilmuir	B.3	V	Kilmuir House	67
Ord	C.4	V	Fiordhem	44

INTRODUCTION

WHY SCOTLAND?

If enjoyment of country and wild places is what you most want from a holiday, Scotland is unexcelled.

There are, of course, also innumerable sports like golf and fishing, entertainments such as the Edinburgh Festival, and historic buildings too; but it is the scenery that brings most visitors here – to motor, walk or bicycle. Mountain or moor, sea or loch: all is outstanding.

Most people know that. But it may come as a surprise to learn, as we did when preparing this book, that Scotland is also a gourmet's mecca. Its produce (Angus beef, salmon and trout, raspberries and cheeses) is superb; and in recent years it has inspired some outstanding cooking: flip through the following pages for descriptions of meals in even simple bed-and-breakfast houses and your mouth will begin to water. So many lochs in addition to the sea mean an abundance of fish in great variety.

As to the accommodation described in this book, each has its own distinctive Scottish character: old hunting-lodges and manses, former fishermen's or crofters' cottages, working farms . . . We have sought out those that combine (usually) a historic story with modern comforts and attractive décor, and – in a great many cases – a spectacular view of the sea or a remote glen or mist-capped mountain. Sometimes there are deer or otters or eagles to be seen in the grounds, a frothing beck or waterfall, against a backdrop of purple heather or golden gorse.

New high-speed rail routes get you across the border so quickly that a long weekend may be a practical possibility, even from the south. By car, use the *England and Wales* edition of this book to find a good stopover en route, in order to arrive relaxed and able to enjoy the discoveries that await you. (Order form on page 132.)

This new book about Scotland follows the same lines as the long-established *Staying Off the Beaten Track in England and Wales*, now in its 14th annual edition. Many readers of the latter asked for a Scottish version, and a number even provided recommendations of their own 'finds', which have been of great help – more would be most welcome for the next edition.

Going to Scotland from England has a distinct feel of 'going abroad': a different history, different laws and churches. Old customs and even many sports differ. It helps to know a little about the stormy past that made Scotland what it is – take with you books such as those listed on page xxiv. The terrain is very different – few motorways, on the one hand, and, on the other, little of the network

xvii

of tiny lanes characteristic of England. Don't underestimate the far greater distances to be travelled, going round great mountains and vast lochs.

Though the Highlands are famed worldwide, you need not go so far as that to find spectacular scenery: for instance, just across the border is the Galloway Forest Park with 2000-foot peaks, waterfalls, gorges and moors – contrasting with subtropical plants that come as a surprise on shores washed by the warm Gulf Stream. It is in this region that a plethora of castles and ruined abbeys testify to the drama of Scottish history. For the wildest area in all Britain, however, you have to go to the extreme north (Caithness and Sutherland), motoring along narrow and deserted roads through the grandeur of a landscape carved from some of the world's oldest rocks to a rugged coastline that is indeed utterly 'off the beaten track'.

One holiday will not suffice: Scotland, two-thirds the size of England and full of contrasts, needs repeated explorations.

Auchinlillylynn Spout

In the following pages, the letters NTS stand for the National Trust for Scotland, based at 5 Charlotte Square, Edinburgh, EH2 4DU. Membership of the National Trust entitles you to entry to NTS properties, and vice versa.

Is your surname Leslie? If so, did you know that a Leslie Clan Gathering is planned for 16–18 June 1995 at Leslie Castle in the village of Leslie, 30 miles north-west of Aberdeen, to celebrate 925 years of Leslie association with the site? For further information, contact Leslie Gathering '95, c/o Leslie Castle, Leslie, by Insch, Aberdeenshire, AB52 6NX (tel: 01464 20869).

READER PARTICIPATION

1 It would be very helpful if you will let us know your opinion of places from this book at which you have stayed. Please post this to: Nancy Webber, 35 Winsley, Bradford-on-Avon, Wiltshire, BA15 2LT (no phone calls please!). **If you wish for an acknowledgment please enclose a stamped addressed envelope.**

   Names of establishments   **Your comments (with date of stay)**

2 If you find other houses in Scotland you think we should visit, for possible inclusion in a future edition, please will you send us your description (including price and address), with brochure. **No expensive places, please.** See overleaf.

   Your name and address (capitals):_____
   _____

   Date:_____ Occupation (optional):_____

PROPRIETORS WISHING TO APPLY FOR INCLUSION: see overleaf.

THANK YOU...

to those who send details of their own finds, for possible future inclusion in the book. Do not be disappointed if your candidate does not appear in the very next edition. We never publish recommendations from unknown members of the public without verification, and it takes time to get round each part of Scotland in turn.

Inevitably, there is a time-lag between visits and the appearance of what is written in book form. The details you send will be filed, under regions, until such time as we go to the region in question; and then they will be a very great help, although there will not necessarily be enough space for all of them to be used. Please, however, do not send details of houses already featured in many other guides, nor any that are more expensive than those in this book.

> **At houses where dinner is not served, a light supper can often be obtained (if ordered in advance), ranging from sandwiches to family 'pot luck'. (Packed lunches too.) Price from about £2 to £8.**

'**NO VACANCIES**' It is unreasonable to expect to find vacancies (particularly the least expensive rooms) at short notice. Book as early as you can, especially for times when your chosen area is likely to be full of visitors (e.g. for the Highland Gathering at Braemar).

> ## APPLYING FOR INCLUSION IN
> ## *STAYING OFF THE BEATEN TRACK*
>
> Proprietors who would like their houses to be considered for a future edition of this book are welcome to apply, particularly if in areas not already well covered; *provided that* the b & b price is within the book's limits (see page xxii). Ideally, either dinner or light snacks should be available in the evening. There is no charge for an entry but, compiling the book being expensive, nearly all proprietors make a contribution at the end of each year (no bills are issued). Every house has to be visited first and it may be some time before this takes place. Brochures, prices, menus, etc. should be posted to: Nancy Webber, 35 Winsley, Bradford-on-Avon, Wiltshire, BA15 2LT. **No phone calls please.**

HOW TO HAVE A GOOD TIME

Some people have very particular requirements; and it is up to them to discuss these when telephoning to book. Many hosts in this book are more flexible than big hotels, and all are eager to help if they can. We have in mind such things as: a bad back, needing a very *firm mattress* (folding backboards are available from the Back Shop, tel: 0171-935 9120); special *dietary* requirements, and *allergies* to feather pillows or animals; a strong preference for *separate tables* rather than a shared dining-table – or vice versa; *fewer courses* than on the fixed menu; *twin beds* rather than double beds – or vice versa; freedom to *smoke* – or freedom from it; a particular wish for *electric blanket, hot water bottle*, etc., or a dislike of *duvets*; the need to arrive, depart or eat at *extra-early* or *extra-late* hours; an intention to pay by *credit card* (this should not be taken for granted, particularly at small guest-houses).

The code letters that appear after the name of each house will help you identify houses suitable for children, dogs, people with mobility problems, users of public transport, etc.: for full explanation, see page xxviii. Please also use the 'how to book' checklist on page xxii when telephoning.

It's best to stay at least 2–3 days: you cannot possibly appreciate an area if you only stay overnight (prices per night are often less, too, if you stay on). The vouchers on page ii are usable for 3-night stays. At some houses, 1-night bookings may be refused.

There is another important component in having an enjoyable experience: congenial company. Many readers have commented that, when they stay at a house recommended in *Staying Off the Beaten Track*, they find other visitors – also readers – very agreeable company because they are compatible people.

When to go? Seaside resorts or other places suitable for children will be at their busiest (and dearest) during school holidays (in Scotland, the month of July). Other peak periods are, of course, Easter, Christmas and Hogmanay (New Year's Eve). There are local peaks, too (the Edinburgh Festival or the major golf tournaments at St Andrews, for instance, are apt to fill hotels for miles around). In holiday areas, travel on any day other than a summer Saturday if you can. Make ferry, Motorail or coach/train reservations well in advance. And if you plan to come home with presents for yourself or your family and friends, take with you *The Factory Shop Guide for Scotland* (available from 1 Rosebery Mews, Rosebery Road, London, SW2 4DQ, tel: 0181-678 0593), featuring 100 shops selling a huge variety of items.

TELEPHONING TO BOOK: A CHECKLIST

Book well ahead: many of these houses have few rooms. Further, at some houses, rooms (even if similarly priced) vary in size or amenities: early applicants get the cheapest and/or the best ones. Mention that you are a reader of this book: sometimes there are discounts on offer exclusively for readers. Telephoning is preferable to writing to inquire about vacancies, and, in many cases, the best time is early evening.

1. Ask for the owner by the *name* given in this edition. (If there has been a change, standards and prices may differ.)
2. Specify *your precise needs* (such as en suite bathroom, if available), see page xxi. (Do not turn up with children, dogs or mobility problems if you have not checked that these are accepted or provided for.) Elderly people may wish to ensure that their room is not on the second floor.
3. Check *prices* – these, too, can change (particularly after spring). Ask whether there are any bargain breaks.
4. Ask what *deposit* to send (or quote a credit card number). Overseas visitors may be asked to pay up to 50%.
5. State your intended *time of arrival*, what meals are wanted and at what times. (If you should then be late, telephone a warning – otherwise your room may be let to someone else. It is inconsiderate to arrive late for home-cooked meals prepared especially for you.) Most proprietors expect visitors to arrive about 5pm. In country lanes, finding your way after dark can be difficult.
6. Ask for precise instructions for *locating the house*: many are remote. Better still, ask for a brochure with map to be posted to you.
7. Few proprietors expect visitors to stay out of the house in the daytime; but if you want to stay in, check this when booking.

PRICES

Staying Off the Beaten Track came into being to provide a guide to good accommodation at prices suited to people of moderate means. That remains its policy.

In the current edition are houses at which it is possible to stay, at the time of publication, for as little as £11–£20 for b & b – that is, per person sharing a double room. (However, for the best rooms in the house, or later in the year, you may well be asked for more. **Check when booking.**) You can see from the text when price rises occur.

The prices are as quoted to us when the book was in preparation during 1994. But sometimes unexpected costs force proprietors to increase their prices subsequently: becoming liable for VAT or business rates, for instance.

Inclusive terms for dinner, bed and breakfast (particularly for a week) can be much lower than those quoted here for these items taken separately. Many houses in this book have bargain breaks or other discounts on offer, some exclusive to readers. A 'bargain break' is usually a 2- or 3-day booking including dinners, at a discount; sometimes at low season only.

HOW TO GET TO SCOTLAND

By car   Major routes are: M6 – Carlisle – A74 towards Edinburgh and Glasgow; M6 – Carlisle – A7 to Edinburgh; M1 – M18 – Darlington – A68 to Edinburgh; A1 – Berwick-upon-Tweed – east-coast route to Edinburgh.

London to Edinburgh is 378 miles; to Glasgow, 397 miles. For stopovers en route, see *Staying Off the Beaten Track in England and Wales* (order form on page 132).

By coach   National Express runs coaches to Glasgow and Edinburgh from 'almost everywhere'. For timetables, contact National Express, 4 Vicarage Road, Birmingham, B15 3ES (tel: 0121-456 1122).

By rail   At the time of going to press, InterCity passenger services ran from King's Cross to Edinburgh, Glasgow, Perth, Inverness, Dundee and Aberdeen (the 'east coast' line); and from Euston to Glasgow and Fort William (the 'west coast' line). InterCity Motorail – for cars as well as passengers – ran day and night services from London to Glasgow; night services from London to Edinburgh, Fort William, Inverness and Aberdeen; and a night service from Bristol to Edinburgh (sleepers available on night services). For timetable, contact InterCity Motorail, Box 44, Edinburgh, EH1 1BA (tel: 0345 090700).

WITHIN SCOTLAND

There are coach services from Glasgow and Edinburgh to all major towns and most smaller ones. Timetables available from Tourist Information Centres, or contact Caledonian Express, tel: 0141-332 4100 (Glasgow) or 0131-452 8777 (Edinburgh).

ScotRail's scenic West Highland line celebrated its centenary in 1994. It covers over 200 miles of spectacular countryside between Glasgow, Fort William, Mallaig and Oban. For information on this and other routes contact ScotRail, 58 Port Dundas Road, Glasgow, G4 0HG (tel: 0141-335 2244).

The Royal Mail's Postbus service comprises a fleet of minibuses and cars which collect and deliver mail and carry passengers at a modest cost on more than 130 routes through many of the most beautiful areas of Scotland. Local timetables available from post offices and Tourist Information Centres, or contact Post Office Public Affairs, 30 St James's Square, London SW1Y 4PY, or Royal Mail Public Relations, 102 West Port, Edinburgh, EH3 9HS.

Caledonian MacBrayne Hebridean and Clyde Ferries operate between more than 50 different ports or terminals on the mainland and over 20 islands. For information, contact Caledonian MacBrayne, Gourock, PA19 1QP (inquiries: 01475 650100; reservations: 01475 650000).

BOOKS TO READ

One of Scotland's finest historians is an Englishman who grew up in Canada: journalist and writer John Prebble. He has written at length on *Glencoe*, *Culloden* and *The Highland Clearances* (all available in Penguin), and the richly illustrated *John Prebble's Scotland*, out of print but available in libraries, bears comparison with Alistair Cooke's *America* (though browsers might be frustrated by the lack of an index). And his *The Lion in the North* (Penguin) is one of the most readable single-volume histories of Scotland available.

It is not the only commendable history, however: J. D. Mackie's *A History of Scotland* (Penguin) and Rosalind Mitchison's work of the same title (Routledge) both received excellent reviews; and *Scotland: A New History* by Michael Lynch (Pimlico) looks set to become a standard work. Fitzroy Maclean's *Scotland: A Concise History* (Thames & Hudson) is persuasively written and beautifully illustrated. Finally, George MacDonald Fraser, author of the brilliant *Flashman* novels, has written the story of the Anglo-Scottish Border reivers (or robbers), who flourished until the Union of the Crowns in 1603, in *The Steel Bonnets* (Harvill).

Antonia Fraser's scholarly and exhaustive *Mary Queen of Scots* (Mandarin) remains one of the best studies of that ill-fated lady, but for those looking for a less demanding acount of her tragic life an American, Margaret George, has written a well-researched novel *Mary, Queen of Scotland and the Isles* (Pan). The excellent novelist Margaret Irwin has told the stories of two other romantic figures from Scottish history in *The Proud Servant* (Montrose) and *The Gay Galliard* (Bothwell), both now out of print but still to be found in libraries and secondhand bookshops.

There are biographies of Charles Edward Stuart by Margaret Forster (*The Rash Adventurer*) and Fitzroy Maclean (*Bonnie Prince Charlie*, published by Canongate), and of the Marquis of Montrose by Max Hastings, C. V. Wedgwood, Ronald Williams and Violet Wyndham.

For local colour, take the novels of Sir Walter Scott and Robert Louis Stevenson and the poetry of Robert Burns; and above all remember to pack the all too imitable *Poetic Gems* of William McGonagall (Duckworth), poet, tragedian and unbelievably funny.

Facts (prices, etc) at the top of entries are supplied by the proprietors themselves. While every effort is made to ensure that these are correct at the time of going to press, they may alter thereafter; please check when you book.

THE SCOTTISH WILDLIFE TRUST

The Scottish Wildlife Trust is a young and thriving organisation, born in the 1960s and taking on the environmental problems of the 1990s. It is the largest voluntary body working for wildlife conservation in Scotland and owns, runs or helps manage over 80 wildlife reserves where animals, birds and wildflowers can flourish in peace and safety. The aims of the Trust are:

- to establish and manage wildlife reserves
- to influence society by campaigning on relevant issues and providing quality advice to local authorities, landowners and others
- to raise public awareness so that everybody can contribute positively to the conservation of Scotland's natural heritage
- to carry out surveys and maintain records of Scotland's wildlife resources and their distribution.

Within the UK, SWT is a partner in the largest British voluntary wildlife body, the Royal Society for Nature Conservation Wildlife Trusts Partnership: a collection of 47 Trusts, locally and nationally linked. Children can join SWT's junior wing, WATCH Scotland. WATCH tackles projects of international importance like measuring acid rain and ozone levels, and checking the health of Scotland's rivers.

SWT believes that one of the best ways to protect wildlife is to buy important natural habitats. Once in SWT's ownership, the land is safe from further development and can be carefully managed for the benefit of wildlife. There are informative visitor centres at the Falls of Clyde in Lanarkshire (nearest b & b houses, **Glentewing Farm, Netherton Farm** and **Townfoot**), the Loch of Lowes by Dunkeld (nearest houses, **Upper Woodinch** and **Bheinne Mhor**) and St Abb's Head (nearest houses, **Castle Rock Hotel, Harelawside** and **St Albans**). A flagship centre is due to open in 1995 in the Montrose Basin (nearest house, **Kirkgate House**). There are many other established reserves, where examples of all of Scotland's major natural habitats are protected, from rocky coastline to old woodland and upland.

Your support will help SWT to manage these reserves and buy more land too. Benefits of membership include:

- the satisfaction of supporting positive action on behalf of wildlife in Scotland
- the opportunity to learn more about wildlife and join in local activities
- access to SWT's wildlife reserves, visitor centres and hides
- free copies of the magazine *Scottish Wildlife*, published three times a year.

To join, see over

SWT MEMBERSHIP APPLICATION

Please tick the appropriate box   per annum

Ordinary	£15 ☐
Family	£25 ☐
*Family & WATCH	£25 ☐
WATCH (Junior SWT)	£5 ☐
Senior Citizen	£9 ☐
Family Senior Citizen	£15 ☐
Unwaged	£6 ☐
Student	£6 ☐
Life	£320 ☐
Donation	£_____

* Family & WATCH provides membership of SWT for two adults plus membership of WATCH for up to 4 children living at the same address.

Subscriptions are renewable on the anniversary of joining.
Please make your cheque payable to 'Scottish Wildlife Trust'.

Name _____

Address _____

_____

_____ Postcode _____

Signature _____ Date _____

Children's Names: Ages

1 _____ (   )

2 _____ (   )

3 _____ (   )

4 _____ (   )

Please return this form to:
Scottish Wildlife Trust, Freepost EH858, Edinburgh, EH4 0HX
No stamp is required, but if you use one, it will allow SWT to spend more money on conservation.

HIGHLAND GAMES IN 1995

For nearest b & b houses, see Jedburgh, Kelso and Galashiels (Borders) in regional list, pp xiii-xvi.

Hawick Common Riding	10 June
Selkirk Common Riding Games	17 June

For b & b houses near the following towns, see pp xiii-xvi.

Grantown-on-Spey Highland Games	25 June
Dingwall Highland Gathering	8 July
Jedburgh Border Games	8 July
Tomintoul Highland Games	15 July
Burntisland Highland Games	17 July
Inveraray Highland Games	18 July
St Andrews Highland Games	30 July
Skye Highland Games	2 Aug
Aboyne Highland Games	5 Aug
Montrose Highland Games	6 Aug
Perth Highland Games	13 Aug
Helmsdale Highland Games	19 Aug
Crieff Highland Gathering	20 Aug
Argyllshire Highland Gathering (Oban)	24 Aug
Birnam Highland Games	26 Aug
Edinburgh Highland Games	27 Aug
Braemar Highland Gathering	2 Sep
Blairgowrie Highland Games	3 Sep

Please note that, at the time of going to press, these dates were provisional only. For confirmation, and a complete list of fixtures, contact the Scottish Games Association, 24 Florence Place, Perth, PH1 5BH (tel: 01738 627782).

As part of the celebrations of the 250th anniversary of the last Jacobite uprising, the 50th anniversary Glenfinnan Highland Games will be held on the day Bonnie Prince Charlie raised his standard there against the English: 19 August. Nearest b & b houses **Ardsheal Home Farm, Invergloy House** and **Old Pines**.

EXPLANATION OF CODE LETTERS

(These appear, where applicable, in alphabetical order after the names of houses)

C Suitable for families with children. Sometimes a minimum age is stipulated, in which case this is indicated by a numeral; thus **C**(5) means children over 5 years old are accepted. In most cases, houses that accept children offer reduced rates and special meals. They may provide cots, high chairs and even baby-sitting; or games and sports for older children. Please enquire when booking. And do not expect young children to be lodged free, as babies are. Many houses have playing-cards, board games, irons, hair-dryers, maps, gumboots, bicycles, and so forth – just ask. Families which pick establishments with plenty of games, swimming-pool, animals, etc., or that are near free museums, parks and walks, can save a lot on keeping youngsters entertained. (Readers wanting total quiet may wish to avoid houses coded **C**.)

D Dogs permitted. A charge is rarely made, but it is often a stipulation that you must ask before bringing one; the dog may have to sleep in your car, or be banned from public rooms.

M Suitable for those with mobility problems. Needs vary: whenever we have used the code letter **M**, this indicates that not only is there a ground-floor bedroom and bathroom, but these, and doorways, have sufficient width for a wheelchair, and steps are few. For precise details, ask when booking.

PT Accessible by public transport. It is not necessary to have a car in order to get off the beaten track when public transport is available; houses indicated by the code **PT** have a railway station or coach stop within a reasonable distance, from which you can walk or take a taxi (quite a number of hosts will even pick you up, free, in their own car). The symbol **PT** further indicates that there are also some buses for sightseeing, but these may be few. Ask when booking.

S Indicates those houses which charge single people no more, or only 10% more, than half the price of a double room (except, possibly, at peak periods).

X Visitors are accepted at Christmas, though Christmas meals are not necessarily provided. Some hotels and farms offer special Christmas holidays; but, unless otherwise indicated (by the code letter **X** at top of entry), those in this book will then be closed.

ALPHABETICAL DIRECTORY OF HOUSES AND HOTELS

Prices are per person sharing a double room, at the beginning of the year. You may be quoted more later or for single occupancy.

Prices and other facts quoted at the head of each entry are as supplied by the proprietors.

ACADEMY HOUSE CDS
School Road, Fordyce, Banffshire, AB45 2SJ (Grampian)
Tel: 01261 842743
West of Banff. Nearest main road: A98 from Fochabers to Fraserburgh.

3 Bedrooms. £16–£18. Views of garden, village. Washing machine on request.
Dinner. £10 for 3 courses and coffee at 7–7.30pm. Non-residents not admitted. Vegetarian or special diets if ordered. Wine can be brought in. **Light suppers** sometimes.
1 Sitting-room. With central heating, TV, piano.
Large garden.

Fordyce is an attractive conservation village with a 16th-century castle next to the ancient churchyard; the 14th-century church has been turned into a visitor centre. At Duff House in Banff a country-house extension of the Scottish National Gallery is due to open in 1995, the first of its kind in Scotland; and for romantics, a trip to Pennan Head is a must: Pennan is the village where *Local Hero* was filmed.

Elegant, white-painted Academy House was built as a school in 1846. Thirty-six years later, the school moved to larger premises across the road, and the house was left to combine the functions of home for the headmaster and boarding accommodation for some pupils. By the early 1960s it was empty, and remained so for 15 years. Although it seems incredible now, it was precisely because the house was a black spot in what was otherwise one of the best conserved small rural villages in Scotland that it first came to the attention of Richard Leith, a council planner involved in conservation projects (the fascinating Joiners Workshop museum is his brainchild). With his wife Sandra, a physiotherapist, he bought and transformed Academy House in 1976.

Now there is a rust-coloured carpet in the sitting-room, the chairs are upholstered in cream, with a pattern in blue and rust, and the walls are hung with paintings by Richard and other local artists. More pictures grace the dining-room, alongside Sandra's needlework and Victorian photographs of Richard's grandparents. Upstairs, a huge green-and-coffee-coloured room has bedheads and chair-arms finished with old tapestry; in another room, with flowery fabrics and a half-coronet over the bed, the fretworked bedhead was originally the front of a piano. A third room is decorated in beige and pink to set off the cane bed; the pretty bathroom is green, with stencilling round the walls.

For breakfast, you might be offered cheese, fresh fruit, oatcakes and yogurt besides bacon and eggs; dinner might start with smoked mackerel pâté made with local mackerel, or home-made cullen skink (creamy smoked haddock soup served with oatcakes), followed by local meat or fish, and sticky toffee pudding or syllabub.

ALLTAN
Ferindonald, Teangue, Isle of Skye, IV44 8RF Tel: 014714 342
On A851 from Broadford to Armadale.

rear view

4 Bedrooms. £15–£17 (less for 4 nights). Tea/coffee facilities. Views of garden, country, sea. No smoking.
Dinner. £12 for 3 courses and coffee at 7pm. Non-residents not admitted. Vegetarian or special diets if ordered. Wine can be brought in. No smoking.
Light suppers if ordered.
1 Sitting-room. With open fire, central heating, TV, record-player. No smoking.
Small garden.
Closed from December to February.

Alltan stands high above the single-track A851 between Broadford and Armadale (ferry to Mallaig), but on Skye even a main road would be considered off the beaten track if it were anywhere else.

Janet and Brian Shaw came to Skye in the early 1980s, but found it wasn't as easy to buy land as they had hoped. An indirect result of the scandal of the Highland Clearances was the passing, in 1886, of the Crofters' Holdings (Scotland) Act, under which, for the first time, crofters were to be granted security of tenure, and could pass crofts down through their families. At the same time, a Crofters' Commission was set up to supervise the working of the new legislation. Thus, the Shaws had to reconcile the demands of the landowner, the crofter and the Commission before taking possession of the plot, but it was done at last, and in 1985 they were able to move into their new house.

Bedrooms are not large, but the views ensure an effect of infinite space: from one, across the Sound of Sleat to the head of Loch Hourn; and from the other, over the Sound to Mallaig and the head of Loch Nevis. Between the two lochs is the almost roadless Knoydart peninsula, with several peaks over 3000 feet. Downstairs, a third, pink-and-brown bedroom shares an attractive bathroom with a small room at the back suitable for children.

The apricot-painted sitting-room and the dining-room both look south-east across the Sound to Knoydart, and guests can drink in the view while enjoying Brian's simple, wholesome food like home-made soup, a roast or fish with fresh vegetables whenever possible, and a pudding. For breakfast you might be offered fresh fruit and yogurt.

This southern tip of Skye, the Sleat peninsula, is known as the garden of the island, but besides the beauty of the scenery there are the ruins of Dunsgaith and Knock castles to admire, as well as Armadale Castle with its famous gardens and the Clan Donald Centre, the latter devoted to the history of the Macdonalds of Skye.

ALVIE MANSE
Alvie, Inverness-shire, PH22 1QB (Highland)   Tel: 01479 810248
North-east of Kingussie. Nearest main road: A9 from Inverness to Perth.

3 Bedrooms. £15. Views of garden, country, loch. No smoking. Washing machine on request.
Dinner. £12 for 3 courses and coffee at times to suit guests. Non-residents not admitted. Vegetarian diets if ordered. Wine can be brought in. No smoking.
Light suppers if ordered.
1 Sitting-room. With open fire, central heating, CD-player.
Large garden.

Nestling on the shore of Loch Alvie, next door to the village church, is this delightful white-painted former manse, dating from around 1740 and now owned by the Alvie estate. The present tenants, Helen and Jim Gillies, have decorated and furnished the house to the highest standard.

In the gracious sitting-room, with deep bay-window seat and open fire, huge comfortable chairs and sofas beckon: there are books to read, curious and lovely *objets d'art* to admire, or the peaceful views across the well-wooded garden to contemplate.

Helen serves dinner by arrangement only, producing such meals as home-made soup, venison or trout, and damson roulade or almond-and-apricot pavlova, but a folder in the sitting-room displays menus from a wide variety of nearby restaurants to pore over, and Helen will advise and book your table as required. Breakfast is served – on Spode china – in the blue dining-room which is furnished, like the sitting-room, with handsome antiques and interesting paintings.

Upstairs, guests share an exceedingly pretty bathroom, with pine panelling and a converted storm lantern in place of a more conventional light-fitting. All the bedrooms have fine old furniture and lovely views; an appropriately ecclesiastical note is struck by the arched door of the single room.

Jim, a conservation and recreation officer with the Forestry Commission, also restores and upholsters furniture; some of his footstools are for sale, along with, for example, his carved wooden cheeseboards, a display of which is itself an attractive addition to the charm of the house.

Alvie lies just south of Aviemore, with all the attractions of the Spey Valley and the Cairngorms within easy reach: skiing in winter, walking and climbing in summer, and birdwatching (at the RSPB reserves at Loch Garten and Loch Insh) all year round.

ALYTH HOTEL CDX
Alyth, Perthshire, PH11 8AF (Tayside)   Tel: 018283 2447
East of Blairgowrie. Nearest main road: A926 from Forfar to Blairgowrie.

8 Bedrooms. £20–£35 (less for 4 nights). Bargain breaks. All have own bath/shower/toilet. Tea/coffee facilities. TV. Views of village, river. Washing machine on request.
Dinner. From £8 for 3 courses (with choices) and coffee at times to suit guests. Vegetarian or special diets. Wine can be ordered. No smoking. **Light suppers** if ordered.
1 Sitting-room. With open fire, central heating, piano. **Bar.**

At first glance, you might not realise you have stumbled across something extraordinary as you enter this small, family-run hotel in Alyth village square – the only hotel in Scotland to be a corporate member of the Scottish Wildlife Trust (see page xxv) – but two minutes with Graham Marshall will convince you. He is a true enthusiast for all the area has to offer, and his interest is delightfully infectious: Arthurian legends, standing stones, folk music and real ale tumble over each other in his conversation; and his love of the surrounding countryside transmits itself so that you too want to rush off to see Guinevere's grave at Meigle, or the beautiful Den of Airlie, a Site of Special Scientific Interest.

Graham and Alison offer traditional Scottish food – especially high tea – music and hospitality: one of the best-known folk clubs in the country meets here on the last Friday of every month for a ceilidh which can go on into the small hours (though without the pounding bass which makes other musical evenings so irritating for non-participants). On the menu are steak pie and haggis, tipsy laird (jam trifle with Drambuie) and cranachan; Scottish cheeses are served with oatcakes, and home-made scones and pancakes appear at teatime.

Upstairs, not all the bedrooms have pretty views – though one looks over what the *Sunday Post* called 'the bonniest close in Scotland' – but all are comfortably furnished and spotlessly clean. The sitting-room, which has a magnificent ceiling-rose and moulded cornices, overlooks the burn which runs through the middle of the village and has been known to yield a salmon or two.

The oldest part of the hotel dates from 1772; the front is early Victorian, with an extension added in the 1880s by the bookseller who then leased part of the building. You couldn't wish for a better guide than Graham either to its history or to what to see and do in the area; and Perth, Dundee and St Andrews are all within easy reach.

ARDEN HOUSE C D M S
Bracklinn Road, Callander, Perthshire, FK17 8EQ (Central)
Tel: 01877 330235
Nearest main road: A84 from Stirling to Lochearnhead.

6 Bedrooms. £16–£20 (less for 7 nights). All have own bath/shower/toilet. Tea/coffee facilities. Views of garden, country. No smoking. Washing machine on request.
Dinner. £10 for 3 courses (with some choices) and coffee at 7pm. Non-residents not admitted. Vegetarian or special diets if ordered. Wine can be brought in. No smoking. **Light suppers** if ordered.
2 Sitting-rooms. With central heating, TV. No smoking.
Garden.
Closed from November to March.

There is a distinct sense of *déjà vu* as you stand at certain windows of Arden House and look down at Callander spread out among the trees below. The very name Arden House might already have set associations whirring – a lilting signature tune, perhaps, or the vision of a tiny grey-haired tyrant in a housekeeper's overall – then one blink and the town below is no longer Callander but Tannochbrae, and you are firmly on the set of the original TV series of 'Dr Finlay's Casebook'. This is the house where the dictatorial Janet ruled with a rod of iron over the hapless doctors Finlay and Cameron in the 1960s, while the BBC's countless viewers looked on.

Today, however, there is no hint of the benevolent-seeming despotism which obtained here, in fiction, for so many episodes. Jim and Dorothy McGregor are kind and considerate hosts and the furnishings of the bedrooms (two on the ground floor) display a lightness of touch with which the no-nonsense Janet could have had little to do. Pink fabrics predominate, flowered or subtly teamed with green or blue, while the sitting-room has William Morris curtains and a variety of comfortable chairs and sofas to choose from. This room, and bedroom no. 6, look out to the Menteith Hills in the south-west; the television room has the familiar view of 'Tannochbrae', while to the west is Ben Ledi, between Callander and the Trossachs. Several paintings of Africa by Jim's aunt, who lived there for some years, hang on the walls of the sitting-rooms.

In the dining-room, with its pine-panelled walls, blue flowery curtains and blue carpet, porridge and oatcakes are usually on offer for breakfast. Dinner might start with cream of cauliflower and almond soup or venison pâté, with salmon or pork (roast or with apricot sauce) to follow and sticky toffee pudding or butterscotch meringue pie to finish.

ARDSHEAL HOME FARM C
Kentallen, Argyll, PA38 4BZ (Highland) Tel: 01631 74229
(from April 01631 740229)
South-west of Fort William. Nearest main road: A828 from Kentallen to Connel.

3 Bedrooms. £14.50–£16. Prices go up in May. One has own bath/toilet. Tea/coffee facilities. Views of garden, country. No smoking.
Dinner. £12 for 3 courses and coffee at 6.30pm. Non-residents not admitted. Wine can be brought in.
1 Sitting-room. With central heating, TV.
Large garden.
Closed from October to March (but open for New Year **to readers of this book only**).

It was a famous 18th-century murder on the Appin peninsula that gave Robert Louis Stevenson the idea for his novel *Kidnapped*, 'the one I'm proud of and that I delight in'. And only a few miles away is Glen Coe, where in February 1692 thirty-eight members of the clan Macdonald (including women, children and an old man of 80) were massacred by a troop of Highlanders commanded by Campbells. It was a political act, designed to subdue the independent Highland chiefs, but the echo of the bitter feud it inspired persists to this day. More happily, a new visitor centre at the foot of the glen celebrates the Highlands of pre-history and folk tales.

Ardsheal is a hill farm, raising sheep and cattle, and surrounded by glorious scenery. Wildflowers are at their best in May and June, and you can wander down wooded paths to the farm's private beach on the shore of Loch Linnhe. The farmhouse is attractively furnished, with antiques in the white-walled sitting-room and a huge scrubbed pine table in the kitchen, where guests have breakfast. Flavia MacArthur does not always serve dinner, but recommends the Holly Tree or the Duror Inn, both less than a mile away, or an excellent fish restaurant at Port Appin. On nights when dinner is available it might be smoked mackerel pâté, pork chops or local trout, and a pudding like apple pie or rhubarb crumble.

There are fresh flowers and pretty fabrics in the bedrooms, one of which has an orthopaedic mattress on a big brass bedstead; bathrooms are roomy and light.

Within easy reach are a National Trust for Scotland Visitor Centre at Glen Coe, Appin Wildlife Museum and a sea-life centre, and lovely gardens to visit up and down this temperate west coast, famous for rhododendrons and azaleas. Riding can be arranged.

ARNISH COTTAGE
Poll Bay, St Catherines, Argyll, PA25 8BA (Strathclyde)
Tel: 01499 302405
East of Inveraray. On A815 from Cairndow to Dunoon.

3 Bedrooms. £18–£22 (less for 4 nights). All have own bath/shower/toilet. Tea/coffee facilities. Views of garden, country, loch. No smoking. Washing machine on request.
Dinner. £12 for 3 courses and coffee at 7pm or times to suit guests. Non-residents not admitted. Vegetarian diets if ordered. Wine can be brought in. No smoking. **Light suppers** if ordered.
2 Sitting-rooms. With open fire, central heating, TV. No smoking.
Small garden.

Although a main road runs behind the house, traffic is screened from view by a tall hedge – an effective sound barrier too – so that Arnish Cottage, a Christian guest-house nestling on the shore of Loch Fyne 20 feet from the high water mark, feels as far off the beaten track as many places much more remote. It is built on the site of an old shepherd's cottage, using stone from the original dwelling.

Poll Bay (from the Gaelic *Creag a' Phuill* – a place of rock pools) is on the eastern shore of the loch, so sunsets are spectacular, and many guests spend summer evenings not moving from the blue-carpeted conservatory, relaxing in the well-padded cane chairs and watching the sun go down over the water.

The same tranquil view across the loch to Inveraray can be had from all the upstairs bedrooms. Pastel walls contrast with colour-stained wood, and one room has a wood-panelled corner bath. There is one downstairs bedroom, with burgundy shower-room, for those who find stairs difficult.

Maisie Mercer is an accomplished cook, producing meals like smoked mussel salad or broccoli soup, salmon with strawberry sauce or roast venison and potatoes rolled in oatmeal, fresh fruit pavlova or 'cornucopia': pastry filled with garden fruit, custard and cream. For breakfast, there might be oatmeal porridge and Loch Fyne kippers – both rare treats. And since the dining-room, too, looks out over the loch, you might spot seals, swans or eider duck on the water.

Loch Lomond is not far away – via the endearingly named 'Rest and Be Thankful' pass – and Glasgow Airport is less than an hour's drive. In Inveraray, the Whisky Shop offers over 400 varieties.

Readers' comments: Delightful situation, very hospitable owners, superb accommodation.

ASHDENE HOUSE
23 Fountainhale Road, Edinburgh, EH9 2LN   Tel: 0131-667 6026

5 Bedrooms. £20–£22 (less for 3 nights). Prices go up at Easter. All have own shower/toilet. Tea/coffee facilities. TV. Views of garden, city. No smoking.
1 Sitting-room. With central heating. No smoking.
Garden.

Touring streets to the south of Edinburgh's Old Town, you can find classical lodges, Victorian baronial mansions, flamboyant public buildings, and some striking modern architecture of Edinburgh University and of the huge Commonwealth swimming-pool. Here once lay the Grange estate, owned by supporters of Mary Queen of Scots; and when the Daulbys first lived at Ashdene House, one of the sandstone houses later built on the estate, they had to pay a feu (feudal dues) to the same family.

The house is an ideal choice if you want not only a very hospitable welcome from Eveline and complete quiet but ready access to the city centre (ten minutes by bus). It is particularly well-placed for visiting Holyrood Palace and its craggy park (some bedrooms have a glimpse of 800-foot Arthur's Seat towering over the park), a choice of golf courses, 15th-century Craigmillar Castle (Mary Queen of Scots once lived here), the Royal Observatory (open to the public) as well as, of course, the city centre itself, particularly the Old Town at the foot of the great 14th-century castle on its precipitous, 400-foot crag. Here is a network of mediaeval courtyards and byways (wynds) to explore, alongside the Royal Mile – a ridgeway connecting the castle with Holyrood Palace, the road flanked with historic houses and speciality shops: it could take a whole day to explore. St Giles Cathedral is here and several of the city's most popular sights – such as the Camera Obscura, Gladstone's Lane (a historic home), the Museum of Childhood, the Whisky Heritage Centre and the People's Story – telling the life of Edinburgh.

You do not need a car in order to explore Edinburgh; which – being only 4¼ hours by train from London – makes it a possibility for southerners to come on even a short break.

Ashdene, a dignified sandstone house once the home of an Edwardian doctor, has bedrooms in shades of pink, many with big armchairs from which to enjoy not just TV but views of the Pentland Hills or the Royal Observatory, and all immaculately kept. Beyond a conservatory breakfast-room is a small garden frequented by squirrels and foxes. There are many restaurants within five minutes - and a good library next door. Eveline is a very helpful adviser on sightseeing.

AUCHENLECK FARM   C
Minnigaff, Newton Stewart, Wigtownshire, DG8 7AA
(Dumfries & Galloway)   Tel: 01671 402035
North-east of Newton Stewart. Nearest main road: A712 from Newton Stewart to New Galloway.

3 Bedrooms. £17–£17.50. All have own bath/shower/toilet. Tea/coffee facilities. Views of garden, country. No smoking.
1 Sitting-room. With open fire, central heating, TV, video, piano.
Large garden.
Closed from November to Easter.

The Scottish nobility have always been keen on shooting, and many an isolated country house was originally a shooting-lodge. This is one such, built by the Earl of Galloway in 1863. It has the conical-roofed turret and crowstep gables typical of the style that Osbert Lancaster dubbed Scottish Baronial. Now the house serves a farm, where the Hewitsons keep sheep and beef cattle.

The turret contains only a spiral staircase. This leads to the bedrooms, each with matching furniture, which look across garden or pasture to the surrounding woods only a field or two away.

Downstairs, there are deep velvet armchairs in the brown and beige sitting-room, and Victorian mahogany furniture in the dining-room. Here Margaret Hewitson serves only breakfast, with home-made preserves, but she does offer packed lunches (including home-made soup and salad vegetables from the garden). Thus provided, one could disappear into the forest for the whole day.

The forest is part of the Galloway Forest Park, 250 square miles of commercial conifers and old mixed woodland managed by the Forestry Commission with considerable attention to its recreational and wildlife importance. Much of it is a nature reserve where wild goats and deer – red, roe, and fallow – may be seen. From the Bruce Stone (marking the defeat of the English in 1307), there is a spectacular view of Loch Trool far below. Cars can go no further than this, but a four-mile walk will take you to the top of Merrick (2766 feet), southern Scotland's highest summit.

For evening meals, the relatively bright lights of Newton Stewart are about five miles away, down a mostly narrow but level and quite straight road bounded by drystone walls, with the forest on one side.

Readers' comments: I found it excellent, very friendly, a high standard of accommodation.

AULTMORE HOUSE
C(12) D PT S X
Nethybridge, Inverness-shire, PH25 3ED (Highland)
Tel: 01479 821473
South of Grantown-on-Spey. Nearest main road: A95 from Boat of Garten to Grantown-on-Spey.

8 Bedrooms. £16–£25 (less for 4 nights mid-week). **10% discount to readers of this book staying 3 nights.** Some have own bath/toilet. Tea/coffee facilities.

Views of garden, country, river. Balcony. Washing machine on request.
Dinner. £7.50 for 3 courses and coffee at times to suit guests. Non-residents not admitted. Vegetarian or special diets if ordered. Wine can be brought in. **Light suppers** if ordered.
3 Sitting-rooms. With open fire, central heating, piano, record-player.
Large garden.
Closed from November to Easter (except Christmas and New Year).

When Arthur and Sheila Edwards started doing bed-and-breakfast at Aultmore House, they used to station themselves at the front door when guests were expected so that they could field those who, after one admiring glance at the impressive façade, would have carried on up the drive towards the garages, unable to believe they could really be heading for such a stately mansion.

However, it is impossible to remain overawed for long in the presence of such warm and informal hosts – although expect a temporary recurrence if you choose the master bedroom, an immense apartment in which the double bed is one of the smaller items of furniture. Its private bathroom is not for those whose taste runs to the modern and pristine: the fittings (including wooden lavatory seat and bone-handled taps) are original, and it boasts an Edwardian bath to dream in, complete with bell-push above the soap-dish. Some might see this as a safety mechanism, but surely, in a more leisured age, it summoned the morning paper, or the second bottle, or a tray of freshly picked peaches from the glasshouse in the walled garden. (In late summer, you might still be offered a home-grown peach after dinner – a meal like steak-and-kidney pudding, or a traditional roast, perhaps followed by treacle pudding.)

The Wilton squares on the parquet floors were made for the house, and, like the curtains, were fitted in such a way as to escape the clutches of the bailiffs who stripped it on the bankruptcy of one owner. Arthur will happily bring you up to date with his research into the house's chequered history, and his progress on its restoration. Designed by Sir Reginald Quennell, Aultmore was built as a second home in 1912, when the late Queen Victoria's love-affair with Balmoral had made summer retreats to Scotland fashionable. The Great War ruined its owner, and its fortunes thereafter seem to have fluctuated alarmingly, reaching their nadir in the hands of the receivers from whom the Edwardses bought it.

AVINGORMACK
Boat of Garten, Inverness-shire, PH24 3BT (Highland)
Tel: 0147983 614
South-west of Grantown-on-Spey. Nearest main road: A95 from Aviemore to Grantown-on-Spey.

4 Bedrooms. £16–£18 (less for 6 nights). Some have own bath/shower/toilet. Tea/coffee facilities. Views of garden, country. No smoking. Washing machine on request.
Dinner. £12 for 3 courses and coffee at 7pm. Non-residents not admitted. Vegetarian or special diets if ordered. Wine can be brought in. No smoking.
Light suppers if ordered.
1 Sitting-room. With central heating, TV, record-player. No smoking.
Large garden.
Closed in November.

To wake up in the morning and draw back the curtains on a prospect of the Cairngorms in all their splendour is a memorable experience: it is easy to see why, instead of the more conventional representations of their house, Jan and Matthew Ferguson sell postcards of 'The View from Avingormack' painted by a local artist.

The guest-house is particularly attractive to those who wish to walk, canoe, sail, fish or play golf; birdwatchers come to see the ospreys at the RSPB reserve at Loch Garten. Trips to see the resident dolphins and seals in the Moray Firth can be arranged, and recently Jan has noticed an influx of Europeans who come for the mushroom-picking!

The food here is outstanding: you will be offered freshly baked scones or fruit muffins at breakfast, and spiced fruit compote, with specialities such as crêpes with wild mushrooms. The home-made soup at dinner might be spinach-and-coconut, or courgette-and-mint, or you might start with mille-feuille stuffed with leeks and smoked salmon; the main course might be Spey salmon with orange sauce, local venison baked in red wine, or Scotch lamb with mustard-and-honeycream sauce, all with fresh vegetables, often from the Fergusons' organic garden; pudding might be (if you're very lucky) orange-and-nut bread-and-butter pudding, or steamed date-and-walnut pudding, or home-made ice cream. Vegetarian meals are a speciality.

Jan makes all the furnishings, so bedrooms are bright with Liberty-style or sprigged fabrics; one has peach-striped wallpaper, another a watered-silk effect. All the rooms but one have the view of the Cairngorms; the family room looks onto the equally attractive birch woodlands where those edible mushrooms flourish.

Avingormack probably derives from Norse words meaning 'little green place'; the house, in all senses, lives up to its name.

BALKISSOCK LODGE
Ballantrae, Ayrshire, KA26 0LP (Strathclyde)   Tel: 01465 83537
South-west of Girvan. Nearest main road: A77 from Stranraer to Glasgow.

3 Bedrooms. £20 **to readers of this book only.** All have own bath/shower/toilet. Tea/coffee facilities. TV. Views of garden, country. No smoking.
Dinner. £13–£20 for 3 courses (with choices) or à la carte and coffee at 7–9pm. Vegetarian or special diets if ordered. Wine can be brought in. No smoking.
1 Sitting-room. With open fire, central heating. Piano.
Garden.
Closed from November to March.

Although this Georgian shooting-lodge is set in ideal walking country, with facilities for strenuous activities like pony-trekking and mountain biking readily available, those whose pleasures are of a more sedentary – not to say sybaritic – nature need not despair. Their aim, say Adrian and Janet Beale, is to provide a rest-cure not a route-march, and guests are offered every inducement to take them up on their promise.

Janet, a professional cook and former head of Home Economics at a school in Ludlow, knows the way to her visitors' hearts, and it starts in the dining-room. Here you can choose between the table d'hôte (which always includes vegetarian choices like cheese-and-walnut pâté to start, or spinach-and-mushroom lasagne) or a varied à la carte menu which also features vegetarian options as well as several fish dishes. Main courses might be venison casserole with red wine and prunes, or salmon steak with a citrus dressing; puddings range from the restrained (ice creams, sorbets) to the gloriously self-indulgent like Victorian Whimwham – a Scottish layered trifle. The breakfast menu changes daily, and might include devilled kidneys, a double Dutch pancake (with ham and melted cheese), or banana, cheese and almond kedgeree!

Adrian and Janet came here in 1991, when Balkissock was still divided into two houses. The process of restoration had been going on for a dozen years before that, but the Beales have achieved wonders, creating a cosy sitting-room overflowing with books and pictures and three charming guest bedrooms (named after Impressionist painters) besides that delightful dining-room, with its piano, open fire, and glass door opening onto the garden. One bedroom can be let in conjunction with a pretty single as family accommodation; another has a particularly good cinnamon-carpeted bathroom with poppy paper.

Ballantrae is only a few miles up the coast from Stranraer, so Balkissock is an ideal stopover on the way to or from Northern Ireland. Those who enjoy the good things in life, however, will stay a lot longer.

BARNEY MAINS
Haddington, East Lothian, EH41 3SA (Lothian)
Tel: 01620 880310
Off A1 from Edinburgh to Berwick-upon-Tweed.

3 Bedrooms. £15–£20 (less for 3 nights). Prices go up in July. Tea/coffee facilities. Views of country, sea. No smoking. Washing machine on request.
Light suppers if ordered.
1 Sitting-room. With open fire, central heating, TV, record-player.
Garden.
Closed from December to February.

Convenient though this is for a stopover on the way to Edinburgh, the 18th-century house deserves a longer stay. For over a century the Kerr family have cultivated the main farm on the estate of the Earl of Wemyss and March and lived in this 18th-century house (with later extensions), the deep-shuttered windows of which have views of Barnes Castle – started but never finished by Scotland's 17th-century ambassador to Spain. It is on the site of a hilltop Pictish fort with a panoramic view that embraces the Kingdom of Fife across the Firth of Forth, the Lammermuir Hills and the Bass Rock. Around the house are fields of grain, peas or cows; inside it, a crackling fire and velvet armchairs in a spacious sitting-room with nice pieces of Victorian furniture, a big dining-room (with Egyptian embroideries and old pictures the young Kerrs discovered in the attic) and a prettily balustraded stone staircase leading to the bedrooms. One of these (huge) has a view of the unfinished castle and of a steep gulley with stream, leading to a pond which, when frozen (only once every twenty years!), is used for the Scottish sport of curling. Its other window provides an insight into the private life of house-martins, which nest under its lintel.

Katie Kerr uses the farm's own produce when cooking such Scottish dishes as cullen skink, stovies, whisky-and-honey ice cream or meat marinated in whisky – as well as other popular dishes – lettuce soup, prawn-and-bacon pâté, baked bananas. She makes her own bread and jams, and buys local sausages.

So mild is the climate here that the area is called 'the garden of Scotland'; and it is so historic that Pictish silver treasure has been found (buried when Viking raids occurred), now in Scotland's National Museum. Look for the domed, stone gateposts of fields – an ancient characteristic of the area.

Readers' comments: Extremely interesting and original accommodation. Breakfast excellent; room very clean, warm and comfortable; would certainly go again.

BHEINNE MHOR PT
Birnam, Perthshire, PH8 0DH (Tayside)
Tel: 01350 727779

South-east of Dunkeld. Nearest main road: A9 from Perth to Inverness.

3 Bedrooms. £18–£19 (less for 3 nights). All have own bath/shower/toilet. Tea/coffee facilities. Views of garden, country, village. No smoking.
Dinner. £12 for 3 courses and coffee at 6.30pm. Non-residents not admitted. Vegetarian or special diets if ordered. Wine can be brought in. No smoking.
1 Sitting-room. With open fire, central heating, TV, piano. No smoking.
Small garden.
Closed from mid-December to mid-January.

> *Macbeth shall never vanquish'd be until*
> *Great Birnam wood to high Dunsinane Hill*
> *Shall come against him.*

Just one tree survives from the wood of Shakespeare's day: a venerable oak, beautifully photographed by Peter Buxton as one of a series of exquisite studies which cover the walls of this Victorian house. Fortunately, only one visitor has felt the need to carry a piece of it to Dunsinane Hill (near Dundee) in imitation of Macduff!

Bheinne Mhor (pronounced Ben More) was built at the turn of the century by a prosperous plumber who wanted 'the best-built house in Birnam'. Bedrooms are warm and comfortably furnished, with fresh fruit and flowers to greet each guest; the blue-and-white 'turret room' on the corner of the house is particularly attractive. Downstairs is a green-carpeted sitting-room, with deep green buttoned velvet sofa and chairs and magnolia walls.

Pat, who used to be a ballet teacher in Cheshire and today sings with the Pitlochry choral society, serves dinner by arrangement only, starting perhaps with melon or home-made soup, followed by chicken divan (in a sauce of mayonnaise, curry powder and cheese, on a bed of broccoli) and apple pie or 'tipsy layer': trifle with whisky or Drambuie. Porridge and boneless Arbroath kippers might be on offer for breakfast, and jam and marmalade are home-made.

Macbeth apart, the area is rich in history, not all of it ancient, although Dunkeld, where St Columba's cathedral still stands, used to be the ecclesiastical capital of Scotland. More recently, the Duke of Atholl refused to allow the railway to encroach further onto his land and Birnam became the terminus, growing prosperous as a result; and across the river from the Birnam Oak is Eastwood, where Beatrix Potter wrote *Peter Rabbit*.

BIRKWOOD LODGE
Gordon Crescent, Aboyne, Aberdeenshire, AB34 5HJ (Grampian)
Tel: 013398 86347
Nearest main road: A93 from Aberdeen to Perth.

3 Bedrooms. £18–£20. All have own bath/shower/toilet. Tea/coffee facilities. TV. Views of garden, country. No smoking. Washing machine on request.
Dinner. £15 for 4 courses and coffee at times to suit guests. Non-residents not admitted. Vegetarian or special diets if ordered. Wine can be brought in. No smoking. **Light suppers** if ordered.
1 Sitting-room. With open fire, central heating, piano.
Walled garden.

In a quiet cul-de-sac close to the village centre stands this typical Victorian Deeside house: stone-built, substantial and comfortable. Its pink granite was quarried in Glen Tanar to the south-west; its plasterers, with typical Victorian exuberance, incorporated a pattern of thistles in the elaborate ceiling-rose in the sitting-room, a handsome apartment overlooking the village green which was laid out in 1676. The Aboyne Highland Games are held here on the first Saturday in August, and a pipe-band competition, too.

Upstairs, the two neat front bedrooms (with deep bay windows and prettily tiled shower-rooms) have a grandstand view of the green; at the back, a pink-and-green room has that equally desirable attribute, an attractive bathroom with peony paper, grey-green carpet and white-painted pine-clad ceiling.

On the stairs a painting of his baby brother by Jim and Elizabeth Thorburn's elder son is a fascinating talking-point, but there is so much of interest in the area, and the Thorburns are such friendly hosts, that conversation rarely flags. Elizabeth will tell you of lake dwellings at Loch Kinord, and the Pictish earth house a few miles away which you can explore (with a torch); of Roman forts in the south, and Mount Keen, the most easterly Munro, which was climbed by Queen Victoria. There are capercailzies and ospreys in the Forest of Glen Tanar (part of the old Caledonian Forest); water-skiing and pony-trekking in the countryside; golf, tennis, squash, swimming and rock-wall climbing in the village.

Jim lets fishing on the Dee and does a little estate management, so salmon and sea trout might well appear on the dinner menu; game too. A typical meal might be crab with avocado, roast pheasant with skirlie (an oatmeal dish), cheeseboard (with Stilton) and hazelnut meringue.

BLAIR VIEW   C M S X
Glenshee, Perthshire, PH10 7LP (Tayside)   Tel: 01250 882260
North of Blairgowrie. Nearest main road: A93 from Perth to Aberdeen.

4 Bedrooms. £13.50–£17 (less for 6 nights). One has own bath/shower/toilet. Tea/coffee facilities. TV (in two). Views of garden, country, river. No smoking. Washing machine on request.
Dinner. £9 for 3 courses (with choices) and coffee at 6–8pm. Non-residents not admitted. Vegetarian or special diets if ordered. Wine can be brought in. No smoking. **Light suppers** if ordered.
1 Sitting-room. With central heating, record-player. No smoking.
Large garden.

When the Hardy brothers decided to give up their mushroom farm near Oxford, it was Stan who came north to scout for suitable properties in Scotland. Blair View proved not to be what he was looking for, but he told his brother about it, and in the end Dave and Lynette made the move first, while Stan and Brenda took a little longer to find **Invervar Lodge** (see elsewhere).

Built in 1857, this former farmhouse has been beautifully modernised with outbuildings converted into very comfortable ground-floor accommodation for the Hardys and their guests. Besides a vast blue-and-pink sitting-room, there are two large downstairs bedrooms, one with pine-panelled en suite bathroom, while upstairs are two very pretty rooms with coomed ceilings (in England they would be described as having dormer windows) and an airy bathroom.

For dinner, you might be offered home-made soup or a pasta bake to start, followed by chicken cobbler or beef goulash. Whenever possible, Lynette uses fresh fruit in puddings like crêpes or pastries. Porridge is on offer in the morning, along with the most comprehensive selection of breakfast cereals you are ever likely to encounter! And the house has its own water supply, piped from the surrounding hills.

Views to the south, not surprisingly, are of Mount Blair, while to the north stretches lovely Glenshee, where there are the most extensive downhill skiing facilities in Scotland. (Cross-country skiing may be had in nearby Glenisla.) This is excellent walking country, and the Hardys have a supply of appropriate maps for loan.

Blair View is a mecca for birdwatchers, too: in the course of a summer breakfast, taken by the window in the kitchen/dining-room, you are quite likely to see siskins and other finches, great, blue and coal tits, and pied wagtails only feet away, while ospreys and waterfowl frequent the lochan (small loch) close by.

BLERVIE

C(10) D S X

Forres, Moray, IV36 0RH (Grampian)   Tel: 01309 672358
Nearest main road: A96 from Inverness to Aberdeen.

2 Bedrooms. £20–£25. Prices go up at Easter. Both have own bath/shower/toilet. Views of garden, country. No smoking.
Dinner. £16.50 for 4 courses and coffee at 8pm. Non-residents not admitted. Vegetarian or special diets if ordered. Wine can be brought in. **Light suppers** sometimes.
1 Sitting-room. With open fire, central heating, TV. Piano.
Large garden.

One of the most elegant houses in this book, Blervie is at its best in the autumn, when the creeper which covers the front of the building flames into breathtaking contrast with the warm honey-coloured stone. Built in 1776 as the replacement for Blervie Castle, home of the Dunbar family, which had been destroyed by fire, the house is filled with fine antiques and paintings, a dining-table which will seat 14, and much wooden furniture carved by the Mouse Man, who left his signature in the shape of a mouse somewhere on every piece. There is a lacquered slate fireplace in the dining-room, and the cantilever staircase was salvaged from the castle – the baluster immaculately restored by the local smith. The bedrooms are beautiful, inspiring a hankering for a more gracious age; and – a comforting touch – each bathroom has its own hot water supply, eliminating possible scruples as you sink deep into the roomy, luxurious baths.

The Meiklejohns are hospitable hosts, encouraging guests to dine with them by candlelight, and sharing their wide-ranging interests. Paddy runs field sports courses and is a keen naturalist: he can tell you where to look for ospreys, and reckons his neighbour is the only person in Scotland who can rear capercailzies successfully. One of Fiona's typical dinners might be spinach soup (made from spinach grown in the garden), roast venison with fresh vegetables (also from the garden), fresh pears in fudge sauce, and cheeses.

Besides its magnificent scenery and rich natural history, the area is full of places to see. Brodie Castle and gardens (NTS) are close; Cawdor Castle (Macbeth) is little farther; and even the Culloden visitor centre, a few miles from Inverness, is easily reached. The distilleries of the 'whisky trail' make an interesting tour, as do the coastal villages of this southern coast of the Moray Firth, including Findhorn, Burghead and pretty Portsoy.

2 BONHARD COTTAGES   M S
Bo'ness, West Lothian, EH51 9RR (Central)   Tel: 01506 823938
North of Linlithgow (Lothian). Nearest main road: A904 from Grangemouth to South Queensferry (and M9, junction 3).

2 Bedrooms. £15–£16 (less for 4 nights). Tea/coffee facilities. TV. Views of garden, country. No smoking. Washing machine on request.
Light suppers if ordered.
1 Sitting-room. With wood-burning stove, central heating, TV, record-player. No smoking.
Small garden.
Closed from December to mid-January.

From the window of Monica Caldwell's cosy sitting-room, one can see right down to the road and rail bridges over the River Forth; closer are the topmost roofs of Blackness Castle, once one of the most important fortresses in Scotland. One of only four Scottish castles permitted to keep their fortifications by the Articles of Union, Blackness has since been used as a state prison and in the 19th century as a powder magazine. More recently, Franco Zeffirelli chose the castle as one of the locations for his film of *Hamlet*; one of the places Monica recommends for dinner is the recently rechristened Hamlet in Blackness village, where Mel Gibson and Glenn Close used to relax between sessions. (The Champany Inn is even nearer, and excellent.)

Bonhard Cottages were originally a row of five farm cottages dating from 1906, but were converted into three in the 1960s. The bedrooms are charming, one decorated with a 'poppies' theme, which extends even to the china on the tea-tray, and the other featuring a 'roses' motif. Poppies recur in the neat, quarry-tiled shower-room, too.

Besides being a warm and friendly hostess, Monica is a skilled gardener; vivid pelargoniums line the back porch, tubs spill over with petunias and begonias, and the garden itself is beautifully designed and cared for. Many of the flowers are grown for drying and making into arrangements which Monica occasionally sells to guests.

Pretty Culross (palace, abbey) is close; also nearby is Linlithgow Palace, birthplace of Mary Queen of Scots, where mediaeval banquets are held every August. The House of the Binns (NTS), Hopetoun House and Niddry Castle are all within a few miles, and Edinburgh is close enough to make it very difficult to stay here at Festival time unless you book well ahead (frequent and late-running trains between Edinburgh and Linlithgow mean you don't need to take a car into the city even for evening performances).

BRAERIACH
Kincraig, Inverness-shire, PH21 1NA (Highland)
Tel: 01540 651369
North-east of Kingussie. Nearest main road: A9 from Inverness to Perth.

Tea/coffee facilities. Views of garden, country, river. No smoking. Washing machine on request.
Dinner. £12 for 3 courses and coffee at 7pm. Vegetarian or special diets if ordered. Wine can be brought in. **Light suppers** if ordered.
1 Sitting-room. With open fire, central heating, TV, piano.
Small garden.
4 Bedrooms. £15–£18 (less for 4 nights). All have own bath/shower/toilet.
Closed from November to 27 December.

Braeriach – the 'beautiful hill' – is in fact the third highest mountain in Great Britain: only Ben Macdui (also in the Cairngorms) and Ben Nevis are higher. Weather permitting, its summit is clearly visible from the Johnsons' handsome Victorian manse on the banks of the River Spey, and it seemed natural to name the guest-house after it. On the edge of the pretty village of Kincraig, within easy reach of the A9 which runs virtually the length of Scotland, Braeriach nevertheless feels truly off the beaten track as you look down the garden to the private jetty at the water's edge, then up to the mountains beyond.

To make the most of their situation, Guy has set up a pair of First World War gunsights by the dining-room window to act as powerful binoculars. Otherwise, the room is dominated by a magnificent blonded mahogany dining-table (it once graced a boardroom) where dinner is served on special occasions; usually, guests take their meals nearer the window. Dinner might start with garlic mushrooms or smoked mackerel pâté, followed by local trout, salmon, venison, lamb or beef with fresh vegetables. Much use is made of herbs from the garden, one of Fiona's special interests. Fresh fruit figures largely in the puddings, which might be plum-and-almond pie, spiced peaches (when in season) or profiteroles.

Bedrooms are comfortable and imaginatively furnished, with the freshness of pine panelling and cork tiles much in evidence in the bathrooms; though one smaller shower-room has been papered in silver to increase the perceived size, and very effective this is.

The Spey Valley is almost over-blessed with things to do and see, but most visitors come to Braeriach for the mountains (walking, climbing, cross-country and downhill skiing in winter), the water (salmon in the Spey, a watersports centre on Loch Insh just upriver from the house, and the Johnsons' own canoe for guests' use), or the birdwatching (ospreys on Loch Insh and the RSPB reserve at Loch Garten).

BREADALBANE HOUSE
Main Street, Killin, Perthshire, FK21 8UT (Central)
Tel: 01567 820386
On A827 from Aberfeldy to A85.

5 Bedrooms. £17–£18 (less for 3 nights or continental breakfast). All have own bath/shower/toilet. Tea/coffee facilities. TV. Views of village, country. No smoking.
Dinner. £10 for 3 courses (with choices) and coffee at 7pm. Non-residents not admitted. Vegetarian or special diets if ordered. Wine can be brought in. No smoking. **Light suppers** if ordered.
1 Sitting-room. With central heating, TV.
Small garden.

Breadalbane is the name given to the mountainous area north of Glen Dochart; roughly translated, it means the high country of Scotland. Almost within earshot of the spectacular Falls of Dochart, the pretty village of Killin sits at the head of Loch Tay, where glens converge. Close, too, is Ben Lawers, at nearly 4000 feet one of Scotland's highest mountains. A unique combination of climatic and soil conditions have fostered Alpine plants not found anywhere else in Britain. The mountain is part of a National Nature Reserve, with a visitor centre near Killin.

At Breadalbane House – formerly a bank – Dani Grant offers her guests excellent food and immaculate accommodation: comfortable bedrooms decorated in subtle shades of pink and grey, a blue-and-white dining-room, pot-plants everywhere. For dinner, Dani might serve cauliflower-and-broccoli soup or haggis on toast to start, followed by venison, salmon, or chicken in a honey-and-orange sauce, and finishing with peach-and-ginger cream, a mixed fruit pie, or boozy bread pudding.

Killin is perfectly situated for anyone wanting a central base from which to explore in every direction – Glasgow, Edinburgh, and even Inverness can all be reached within an hour and a half – but for those who do not wish to drive far there is much to enjoy nearer at hand: 'Rob Roy country' and the Trossachs in the south, wild and lovely Rannoch Moor to the north. And in Killin church itself there is a seven-sided font – the only one in Scotland – at least 1000 years old.

> Sir Hugh Munro first published his directory of Scottish peaks over 3000 feet in 1891. Much revised, it now lists 277 'Munros' to be 'bagged', many close to houses in this book.

BRIGHTMONY FARMHOUSE   C
Auldearn, Nairn, IV12 5PP (Highland)   Tel: 01667 455550
East of Nairn. Nearest main road: A96 from Nairn to Forres.

3 Bedrooms. £12.50–£15 (less for 7 nights). Tea/coffee facilities. Views of garden, country. No smoking. Washing machine on request.
Light suppers only.
1 Sitting-room. With open fire, central heating, TV.
Large garden.

This stunning Georgian farmhouse, with its elegantly asymmetric frontage and stone-tiled roof, was built in 1732 as a dower house for the Lethen estate, owned by the Brodie family since the 14th century (Brodie Castle and gardens, now NTS, are near). Margaret and Giles Pearson came here in 1991, and run residential courses in cane and rush seating (Giles is a furniture restorer) as well as offering bed-and-breakfast. Not surprisingly, unusual and beautiful examples of rush and cane furniture are everywhere, some antique, some of Giles's own making, many restored by him. His workshop in the old coach-house is full of work in progress.

The three large bedrooms (which share a sunny bathroom) are all south-facing, with lacy curtains, cane furniture, and views over the garden to the Lethen woods beyond. The sitting-room has comfortable armchairs and walls of the palest green; breakfast is served in the peach dining-room (with log stove). Margaret offers light suppers only, but recommends the excellent restaurant and bar meals at the inn in Auldearn, a mile and a half away.

Also at Auldearn is the National Trust for Scotland's Boath Dovecote (or 'Doocot'), and between Brightmony and the village is Dolmore Manse, where Doris Milton carries on a flourishing antiques business. Auldearn was the scene of a battle in 1645 between Montrose's Highlanders (fighting for Charles I) and the Covenanters, which Montrose won.

This is Macbeth country, too: Forres is where he is said to have met the three witches who hailed him Thane of Cawdor and king hereafter; Cawdor Castle and gardens are near. Also within easy reach are Kilravock Castle and, on the other side of Forres, Kinloss (with abbey), another Brodie stronghold from the 14th century.

> Some proprietors stipulate a minimum stay of two nights at weekends or peak seasons; or they will accept one-nighters only at short notice (that is, if no lengthier booking has yet been made).

BROOMHILL HOUSE C D PT
Navidale Road, Helmsdale, Sutherland, KW8 6JS (Highland)
Tel: 014312 259
On A9 from Inverness to John o' Groats.

3 Bedrooms. £15–£18. Two have own bath/shower/toilet. Tea/coffee facilities. TV. Views of garden, country, sea. No smoking. Washing machine on request.
Dinner. £8 for 3 courses (with choices) and coffee at times to suit guests. Non-residents not admitted. Vegetarian or special diets if ordered. Wine can be brought in. No smoking. **Light suppers** if ordered.
1 Sitting-room. With central heating, TV, piano, record-player.
Small garden.
Closed from November to February.

You will be left in no doubt as to the nature of the hills from which Broomhill House draws its water as soon as you turn on the taps: the rich, brown, peaty brew is some of the softest you are ever likely to bath in, and it makes a splendid cup of tea besides. Being directly on the east-coast route north to Wick, John o' Groats and the Orkney ferry, Broomhill is not strictly 'off the beaten track', but bedrooms are double-glazed.

Gold-mining features in the history of Broomhill in more ways than one. In 1869 the Strath of Kildonan saw the great Sutherland gold rush (and visitors can still pan for gold today); and it was a miner returning from the Klondike who added the turret and conservatory to this former croft house. Two of the bedrooms now have bathrooms in the turret, one room on the first floor boasting an enormous hexagonal bath, while across the landing a king-size room has a magnificent view over the Moray Firth (as does the conservatory downstairs).

Sylvia Blance (a Shetland surname) serves, by arrangement only, such dinners as soup, steak-and-kidney pie or locally caught fish, and lemon mousse. Alex, who was the headmaster of the local school until it stopped taking children over primary age, is the treasurer of Timespan, Helmsdale's award-winning heritage centre, and so is a mine of information on local history and places to see. The area is notorious for the brutal Clearances of the early 19th century, when the Countess of Sutherland and her English husband, the first duke, evicted some 15,000 tenants to make way for sheep. Even today the outrage is not forgotten; when a suggestion was put forward some years ago to floodlight the Duke of Sutherland's monument down the coast at Golspie, local feeling ran so high that the proposal was dropped.

BUNRANNOCH HOUSE C D PT S
Kinloch Rannoch, Perthshire, PH16 5QB (Tayside)
Tel: 01882 632407
Nearest main road: A287 from Killin to A9.

10 Bedrooms. £16–£18 (less for 6 nights). Most have own bath/shower/toilet. Tea/coffee facilities. Views of garden, country. No smoking. Washing machine on request.
Dinner. £15 for 3 courses (with choices) and coffee at 7.30–9.30pm. Vegetarian or special diets if ordered. Wine can be ordered. No smoking.
1 Sitting-room. With open fire, central heating, record-player. Bar.
Large garden.
Closed in December and January.

As late as the end of the 19th century, unmarried daughters could still be a drain on a family's resources. Here, on the Innerhadden estate, the Stewart of the time was fortunate in being able to provide for his: he built a house-cum-shooting-lodge for them.

Keith and Jennifer Skeaping came here in the late 1980s, and have created a delightful atmosphere in this unusual house. On entering, one climbs straight to the first floor (the ground floor, once servants' quarters, is now the family's domain) and into a quiet, comfortable sitting-room, with chairs drawn up round the log fire and lovely views over the wooded grounds. The adjoining dining-room has pale lilac walls that blend subtly with peach and white table linen and polished glassware, promises of delights to come. For, in the former butler's pantry, Jennifer prepares meals which bring her guests back time and again: starters like smoked wild salmon from the Tay served with a salmon mousse, or vegetable soup prepared with home-made pheasant stock; main courses such as fillet steak in a caper, mustard, sherry and cream sauce, or chicken breasts with ginger, peaches and almonds; delectable puddings like apple flan with crunchy almond topping and Drambuie cream, or chocolate sponge log with fresh cream and raspberries. Porridge, muesli and stewed fruit appear at breakfast.

The bedrooms, on the second and third floors, are immaculate, with pastel colour schemes, flowered fabrics, even a cast-iron fireplace in one.

Jennifer, from Australia, is a warm and friendly hostess as well as an inspired cook; Keith works in computers in Edinburgh. They own fishing rights on Loch Rannoch; true to its origins, Bunrannoch is still a haven for sportsmen.

CAIPLIE
53 High Street, Crail, Fife, KY10 3RA Tel: 01333 450564
South-east of St Andrews. Nearest main road: A917 from St Andrews to Kirkton of Largo.

7 Bedrooms. £16.50–£17 (less for 4 nights if dinner is taken, or for continental breakfast). Prices go up in July. Tea/coffee facilities. Views of village, sea. Washing machine on request.
Dinner (to be ordered before 4pm). £12.50 for 3 courses (with choices) and coffee at 7pm. Non-residents not admitted. Vegetarian or special diets if ordered. Wine can be ordered. No smoking.
1 Sitting-room. With open fire, central heating, TV. Bar.
Closed from mid-November to February.

There is a well-known chain of bakers in Fife called Fisher and Donaldson; what is now the dining-room of this homely guest-house was once Mr Fisher's first shop. In those days Crail was still a busy port; today, the village, with its famously pretty harbour, thrives mainly on tourism, though some fishing survives. There is much to see in this East Neuk (or corner) of Fife: the Scottish Fisheries Museum at Anstruther; the splendid church of St Monans (St Monance on some maps); the statue of Robinson Crusoe in Lower Largo, birthplace of Alexander Selkirk (1676–1721), on whose adventures Daniel Defoe is supposed to have based his novel.

Jayne Hudson's cooking is another reason for coming to Crail. At dinner there is always a choice of meat, fish or poultry for the main course; starters might be spiced carrot soup or prawns and onions in cream cheese, while clootie dumpling (a fruit pudding boiled in a cloth) is always one of the choices on the pudding menu.

Decoration throughout the house reflects Jayne's fondness for green: the carpet in the dining-room is that colour, contrasting with cream walls and pale wood tables spread with white lacy cloths. The sitting-room is on the first floor, with green William Morris fabrics and a large-scale map of the East Neuk under the glass top of the coffee table. More maps hang on the walls, and Jayne's collection of old photographs of Crail lines the staircase.

Bedrooms vary in size – one is a single, in cinnamon and green – but for cosy rooms tucked under the roof climb to the second floor, where the largest has a sloping ceiling and Lloyd Loom chairs. There is a shower-room up here, and another on the first floor.

St Andrews is only ten miles away; Edinburgh less than an hour.

Readers' comments: Possibly some of the best food in Scotland. Spotless house; nothing too much trouble for Jayne.

CASTLE ROCK HOTEL D PT S
Murrayfield, St Abbs, Berwickshire, TD14 5PP (Borders)
Tel: 01890 771715
North of Berwick-upon-Tweed (Northumberland). Nearest main road: A1 from Berwick-upon-Tweed to Dunbar.

4 Bedrooms. £20 (less for 5 nights). Prices go up in May. All have own shower/toilet. Tea/coffee facilities. TV. Views of garden, country, sea. Washing machine on request.
Dinner. £13 for 4 courses (with choices) and coffee at 7–7.30pm. Non-residents not admitted. Vegetarian diets if ordered. Wine can be ordered. No smoking. **Light suppers** if ordered.
1 Sitting-room. With central heating, TV, organ, record-player. Bar.
Large garden.
Closed from November to Easter.

Sailors have for centuries called this headland 'the castle' because its crenellated look is so like one. On it, perched right above the foaming sea, was built a Victorian manse (vicarage) with 'gothick' windows, now turned into a small hotel, with dramatic views along a coast of red cliffs and rocks with seabirds – there is a bird and marine reserve at dramatic St Abb's Head, with exhibition. St Abbs itself is a picturesque fishing harbour with lifeboat station.

Peter and Kathryn Lutas (electronics expert and librarian, previously) keep the house immaculately refurbished. The style of furnishing is conventional, with the emphasis on comfort, and most bedrooms have fine sea or harbour views. There is a whirlpool bath for the use of all guests.

Because many visitors (especially those coming straight here from the port or airport of Newcastle) want ideas for touring Scotland, Peter has laid on videos – a different one for every night – that guests can watch on their bedroom TVs, each covering a different aspect of travel in Scotland.

At dinner there is always a choice at each course. A typical meal, cooked by Kathryn, might be potted crab, steak-and-kidney pie, prune syllabub and cheeses.

From here there is a four-mile walk eastward to Eyemouth, via Coldingham and the cliffs: mediaeval kings used to visit Coldingham's great priory, which still stands – an impressive Norman church. Netherbyres is in this direction too, the mansion surrounded by walled gardens. Go the other way and you can see an extraordinary ruin, Fast Castle, perched on a rock-stack in the sea which, in *The Bride of Lammermuir*, Sir Walter Scott called Wolf's Crag; further still is Cove, its harbour far below the clifftop fishing village itself, and Cockburnspath where the Southern Upland Way starts its journey right across Scotland.

CLYNELISH FARM
Brora, Sutherland, KW9 6LR (Highland)   Tel: 01408 621265
Nearest main road: A9 from Inverness to John o' Groats.

3 Bedrooms. £14–£18 (less for 4 nights). Two have own shower/toilet. Tea/coffee facilities. Views of garden, country, sea, river. No smoking. Washing machine on request.
Dinner. £8 for 3 courses and coffee at 7pm. Non-residents not admitted. Vegetarian or special diets if ordered. Wine can be brought in. **Light suppers** if ordered.
1 Sitting-room. With wood-burning stove, central heating, TV.
Large garden.
Closed from November to February.

Next to the telephone in the quarry-tiled hall of this traditional farmhouse (dating from 1865, after the Clearances, when the farm and nearby Clynelish Distillery were built to provide local work for the remaining tenants) stands the visitor's dream: a spanking-new user-friendly computer which will tell you at the push of a button (operated, if required, by Murdo Ballantyne) everything that's happening in the vicinity, where to go, and what to see.

The area is rich in history and interest: there is the world's oldest man-made salmon ladder between Loch Fleet and Loch Buidhe (some of the north's greatest salmon rivers are within a few miles); Europe's biggest guillemot colony up the coast; the Scottish Wildlife Trust reserve at Loch Fleet; fairytale Dunrobin Castle outside Golspie; and, near Bonar Bridge, the site of the Battle of Carbisdale (1650), where the Marquis of Montrose was defeated by the Covenanters, finally forcing Charles II to accept the Scots' demands for presbyterianism if he wanted to be received as king.

The farmhouse is warm and comfortable. In the huge sitting-room, over the blue-and-white tiled fireplace is a beautiful clock set in granite found on the farm, bearing witness to the skill of the Orcadian Stone Company whose workrooms and shop in nearby Golspie are a must for visitors. In the dining-room, with its far prospect over the garden and Clynelish fields to Brora and the Moray Firth, Jane serves, by arrangement only, such meals as home-made soup; a roast, fish, or a casserole, with fresh vegetables; and gooseberry pie. Bedrooms are large, and both they and the bathrooms have splendid views, some over old farm buildings, an old stone laundry, or the 19th-century distillery (now replaced by a modern complex close by). The local supply of soft, brown, peaty water is perfect for both whisky and tea.

COREHEAD FARM
Annan Water, Moffat, Dumfriesshire, DG10 9LT (Dumfries & Galloway)   Tel: 01683 20973

North of Moffat. Nearest main road: A701 from Dumfries to Edinburgh.

2 Bedrooms. £20–£24. Both have own shower/toilet. Tea/coffee facilities. TV. Views of garden, country. No smoking. Washing machine on request.
Dinner (by arrangement). £14 for 3 courses (with some choices) and coffee at 6.30–7pm (later on Sundays). Non-residents not admitted. Vegetarian or special diets if ordered. Wine can be brought in. No smoking. **Light suppers** if ordered.
1 Sitting-room. With wood-burning stove, central heating, TV, video. No smoking. Piano.
Large garden.
Closed from November to February and for lambing.

'A deep, black, blackguard-looking abyss of a hole it is,' wrote Sir Walter Scott in *Redgauntlet*, 'and goes straight down from the roadside as perpendicular as it can.' He was describing the Devil's Beef Tub, a vast natural amphitheatre once used by rustlers as a hiding-place for stolen cattle, and still impressively remote. In the 16th century a stone-built bothy stood at the entrance to the Tub; 200 years later quarters for a married shepherd were built on. John and Berenice Williams came here in the early 1980s, and now the bothy is a low-ceilinged dining-room strikingly decorated in blue and cream, with a piano bearing several trophies for squash and curling, while the 18th-century annexe has been transformed into a cottage-style sitting-room with green walls and carpet and a log-burning stove. On warm summer evenings, though, guests often prefer to linger over their coffee in the quarry-tiled porch, welcoming with its russet walls, and Ercol chairs from which to enjoy the view. Annan Water rises in the Beef Tub, and the valley stretches away in front of the house while the hills rear up behind.

Upstairs, the bedrooms (with roomy showers) are prettily furnished and spotlessly neat, with grey-green carpets and pink or flowered paper; the views, needless to say, are spectacular.

Local produce is used in the kitchen whenever possible, and at dinner the farm's own naturally reared lamb or beef, or locally caught salmon, might follow sausage-stuffed mushrooms or cream of carrot and orange soup. Puddings, like chilled lemon flan or Ecclefechan butter tart, are all home-made.

Corehead is a 2500-acre working hill farm where John keeps a few suckler cows and over 800 sheep; after the lambing, guests are often enchanted by Berenice's pet lambs – piglets too. The magnificent countryside draws walkers and birdwatchers, while Moffat and the trunk road to Edinburgh and Glasgow are only five miles away.

CRAIG HIGHLAND FARM C D M P T S
Plockton, Ross-shire, IV52 8UB (Highland)   Tel: 0159984 205
North-east of Kyle of Lochalsh. Nearest main road: A890 from Strathcarron to Auchtertyre.

3 Bedrooms. £14. One has own toilet. Tea/coffee facilities. Views of garden, country, loch. No smoking. Washing machine on request.
Light suppers if ordered.
1 Sitting-room. With wood-burning stove, central heating, video, record-player.
Large garden.
Closed from January to March.

On the shore of Loch Carron, a few miles from Kyle of Lochalsh and the crossing to Skye, is a real find: a 17-acre rare breeds conservation centre, where bed-and-breakfast guests are welcome to wander around the open farm and see the ancient breeds of Scottish sheep, goats, pigs, llama and ornamental fowl. Seals and even otters have been spotted on the private beach, and there is a heron sanctuary on the small island directly opposite the house.

The two ground-floor bedrooms in the farmhouse have white walls, pine beds and pine-clad ceilings; the family room, reached via a loft ladder, is pine-clad throughout, and – given the slightly unusual access – wisely equipped with its own lavatory and washbasin. There is an attractive bathroom on the ground floor, with shower.

The sitting-room, cosy and glowing in the light of an efficient coal-burning stove, has more white paint and pine, and the roughcast stone wall behind the stove used to be the gable end of the original house.

Vegetarian and vegan breakfasts are available, as well as porridge, kippers, black pudding and home-produced sausage. Patti Heaviside – a midwife – offers light suppers only, but you can eat very well in nearby Plockton (especially at the Plockton Hotel), or at Biadh Math fish restaurant on the station in Kyle of Lochalsh.

From here, popular trips are across to Skye, or over the spectacularly steep and winding road from Kishorn to Applecross, a gem with its stunning bay and view across the Inner Sound to Raasay and Skye. Or you can visit Inverewe Gardens (NTS), a botanic garden to rival any in England. Another NTS property, Lochalsh Woodland Garden, is very close. Plockton itself, known as the jewel of the Highlands, is a picturesque village whose uniform prettiness testifies both to its origins as a planned fishing settlement 200 years ago and to its sheltered position and mild climate: palm trees and flowering shrubs abound.

CROUGHLY FARM
Tomintoul, Banffshire, AB37 9EN (Grampian)
Tel: 01807 580476
South-east of Grantown-on-Spey (Highland). Nearest main road: A939 from Ballater to Nairn.

2 Bedrooms. £14–£15. Both have own bath/toilet. Tea/coffee facilities. Views of garden, country, river. No smoking. Washing machine on request.
Light suppers if ordered.
1 Sitting-room. With open fire, central heating, TV.
Garden.
Closed from October to March.

Listen closely to the Scottish weather reports at the start of any winter and you will probably hear that the A939 from Tomintoul to Cock Bridge is closed. Locals will tell you it is always the first road to become impassable when it snows: driving along it on a fine summer day one is only aware of its absolute beauty. Eastward lie the Ladder Hills; to the south and west lovely Glen Avon stretches to the Cairngorms, some of the highest mountains in Britain; and all around the scenery is breathtaking.

These are the views you will enjoy at Croughly, a working hill farm producing lamb and beef. From the large family room, with windows on three sides, there is not another house in sight, only cattle grazing in the meadows bordering Conglass Water, and the mountains beyond. The 18th-century farmhouse still has its original plaster mouldings and carved wooden jambs round the doors; the bedrooms are comfortably furnished and bathrooms are carpeted and warm.

Anne Shearer serves only breakfast and light suppers in the homely sitting/dining-room; for dinner she recommends any of three restaurants in Tomintoul, two miles away.

The farm is ideally situated for walkers, skiers (Lecht Ski Centre is very near, as well as dry ski slopes at Huntly and Alford), and anyone who just wants to get away from it all; it is also close to the popular Malt Whisky Trail (the farm itself is on the Glenlivet estate) and to the Castle Trail in Gordon District. The attractions of both the Spey Valley and Royal Deeside – especially Balmoral Castle and gardens – are within reach, too.

The Malt Whisky Trail is a 70-mile signposted route round eight famous distilleries in Grampian region. There are guided tours round the centres, and opportunities to buy samples in the gift shops.

CUILMORE COTTAGE   D
Kinloch Rannoch, Perthshire, PH16 5QB (Tayside)
Tel: 01882 632218
Nearest main road: A827 from Killin to A9.

2 Bedrooms. £18–£20. Both have own bath/shower/toilet. Tea/coffee facilities. Views of garden, country. No smoking. Washing machine on request.
Dinner. £22.50 for 4 courses (with choices) and coffee at 7pm. Vegetarian or special diets if ordered. Wine can be brought in. No smoking.
1 Sitting-room. With open fire, central heating. Bar.
Small garden.
Closed from November to January.

Cuilmore Cottage is still so tiny that it is impossible to imagine it as home to a shepherd with 13 children – and that was 65 years ago, before the addition of the upper storey and when the present kitchen was still the byre!

After a brief incarnation as a garage, the kitchen has evolved into the hub around which revolves a successful and highly acclaimed restaurant, built up by Jens and Anita Steffen since they moved here in the late 1970s from Bedfordshire, where Anita taught English. A memorable cook, she now supervises the serving of such superb meals as apple-and-beech-smoked salmon on salad leaves dribbled with hazelnut oil, or seafood risotto glazed with lobster sauce; seasonal soup with freshly baked rolls (all the bread is home-made here); pan-fried venison on a bed of mushrooms and pulses with red wine, or baked fillet of hake in smoky bacon with a chervil-and-lime sauce; and a pudding or Scottish cheeses with home-made biscuits.

The ground-floor of this stone-built cottage dates from 1750, and both the sitting- and dining-rooms are small and cosy, with open fires, old farming implements and family miniatures on the walls of the sitting-room, the original copper hot-water tank in a corner of the dining-room. Guests eat at an old-fashioned scrubbed pine table, thoroughly in keeping with the cottagey ambience.

Upstairs, white paint, pretty fabrics and lots of pine combine with far hill views to give an impression of space in the very attractive bedrooms; the pine-panelled bathroom has a basin ingeniously set into a sewing-machine table. The downstairs bathroom has a bricked-in bath and walls panelled with bleached wood.

For many visitors, this part of Perthshire – Loch Rannoch, Schiehallion and Rannoch Moor – epitomises Scotland. Central enough to be easily accessible, remote enough to remain uncrowded, it is possibly the perfect destination.

DALRACHNEY HOUSE CDS
Carrbridge, Inverness-shire, PH23 3AX (Highland)
Tel: 01479 841250

South-west of Grantown-on-Spey. Nearest main road: A9 from Inverness to Perth.

3 Bedrooms. £17. All have own shower. Tea/coffee facilities. TV. Views of garden, country, river. Washing machine on request. **Dinner.** £10 for 4 courses and coffee at times to suit guests. Non-residents not admitted. Vegetarian or special diets if ordered. Wine can be ordered. No smoking. **Light suppers** if ordered.
1 Sitting-room. With open fire, central heating, TV. Bar.
Large garden.
Closed from November to February.

Less than a year after coming to Dalrachney, Allyson and Tom Jones were welcoming guests back for their fourth visit – drawn, Tom says, by Allyson's cooking, but surely also by the comfort of this Victorian family house, not to mention the possibility of spotting wild cats in the woods behind it. However, a hostess who takes the trouble to gauge whether her guests are likely to prefer wild venison to the farmed variety (less gamy in flavour), and shops accordingly, is bound to be appreciated. A four-course dinner might start with ratatouille or mushroom soup made with cream and fresh herbs (of which there are 52 varieties in the garden); continue with venison cooked slowly in the Aga with heather honey and fresh rosemary, and served with a sauce of honey, rosemary and port, accompanied by fresh vegetables in season; go on with cranachan (fresh fruit, cream and toasted oatmeal) or peaches baked with sugar and brandy; and finish with a selection of English and Scottish cheeses served with oatcakes. Breakfast (cooked by Tom) includes porridge, kippers and black pudding. Bread is sometimes home-baked, jams and marmalade are home-made, and eggs are from the Joneses' free-ranging chickens.

The house itself was built in 1894 by a Scot who had worked in the South African diamond mines; for 30 years it was his family home. It has been a guest-house since the early 1960s, and now the bedrooms are distinguished by the various tartans used in the upholstery and furnishing. Some have the original fireplaces, others attractive, unpainted pitch-pine window-frames. Both the dining-room and the sitting-room have deep bay windows with views over the wooded garden; on chilly evenings the red leather sofa and chairs might be drawn up round a peat fire.

Both Tom and Allyson have a great love and concern for the natural world, and their enthusiasm for their surroundings is infectious, so that their guests are as thrilled as they are when the wild cats deign to appear for a few moments, or a roe deer wanders through the garden.

DAVIOT MAINS FARM   C D X

Daviot, Inverness, IV1 2ER (Highland)   Tel: 01463 772215
South-east of Inverness. Nearest main road: A9 from Inverness to Perth.

3 Bedrooms. £16–£21 (less for 8 nights). Prices may go up in May. Bargain breaks. One has own bath/shower/toilet. Tea/coffee facilities. Views of garden, country. No smoking. Washing machine on request.
Dinner. £10 for 3 courses (with some choices) and coffee at 6.30pm. Non-residents not admitted. Vegetarian or special diets if ordered. Wine can be brought in. No smoking.
1 Sitting-room. With open fire, central heating, TV.
Small garden.

The architecture of Daviot Mains Farm is unusual: its four wings enclose a central courtyard, forming an easily defensible stronghold whose purpose, in a 19th-century farmhouse, is not entirely clear. There are only two others in Scotland built in a similar square, and even the Scottish National Archive can offer Margaret and Alex Hutcheson no explanation for the design.

Inside, the watchword is comfort. The bedrooms – named after local rivers – have sprigged or flowered fabrics and wooden bedheads; one room has a delightfully old-fashioned bath for its own use, while the shared bathroom has a burgundy suite and pink carpet. The sitting-room – where sherry is offered before dinner and home-made cake at bedtime – is furnished with lots of books and deep chairs in which to enjoy them; and a coal-burning stove in the dining-room provides hot water, immediate warmth, and background heating for the whole house.

The food here is exceptional. Dinner (served on week-nights only during the summer, and never on Sundays) might start with home-made soup, or a salad of pears and cheese-stuffed grapes, followed by Loch Ness salmon or chicken almondine (with mushrooms, almonds and a crisp topping). Puddings are delicious, and not for the cholesterol-conscious: Dornoch Dreams are little choux buns filled with cream and raspberries; St Columba's Cream is a mixture of Philadelphia cheese, egg yolk, sugar and vanilla topped with fresh fruit.

Daviot Mains is an ideal base from which to tour the northern Highlands, for Inverness, source of routes in all directions, is only six miles away. Culloden Moor, site of the last battle fought on British soil (in 1746), is even nearer. The battlefield is marked with the initial positions of the armies on both sides, and the visitor centre displays a facsimile of the famous Jacobite order which, reissued by the English with a forged addition denying quarter to English troops, formed the excuse for the barbarities of 'Butcher Cumberland'.

Readers' comments: Highly recommended; bedrooms very pretty and spotlessly clean; Margaret's cooking is exceptional.

DUNDUFF FARM
Dunure, Ayrshire, KA7 4LH (Strathclyde) Tel: 01292 500225
South-west of Ayr. Nearest main road: A77 from Girvan to Ayr.

3 Bedrooms. £15–£20 (less for 6 nights). All have own bath/shower/toilet. Tea/coffee facilities. TV (in two). Views of garden, country, sea. No smoking. Washing machine on request.
Light suppers if ordered.
1 Sitting-room. With open fire, central heating, TV. No smoking.
Large garden.
Closed from October to March.

Dunure was once a fishing port, but its little harbour silted up and is now used only by sailing dinghies. Above it stands Dunduff Farm. The large house, part 15th century and part 17th century, is the heart of a holding now of 700 acres, though it was once even bigger. The Gemmells keep beef cattle and sheep, plus a few more unusual breeds for interest – Highland cattle, for example.

The guests' sitting-room has a huge bay window (its counterpart is in the biggest and best bedroom above). This gives splendid views across the Firth of Clyde, from Ireland on the horizon to the left, to Arran and the Mull of Kintyre. In the middle distance (ten miles out but seeming nearer) is Ailsa Craig, a great dome of granite which was the plug of a vanished volcano. It dominates the seaward view for miles along this coast. You can land on it, weather permitting, to see the lighthouse, the castle – a ruin for 400 years – the smugglers' cave, and the seabirds, from puffins to gannets with six-foot wingspan, and perhaps the wild sheep and goats. At sunset, you can photograph 'the sleeping warrior', whose profile is formed by the rocks and islands.

Another optical illusion is down the road at Electric Brae, where you feel you are going downhill when the road is actually rising. A board by the roadside explains the phenomenon and how it got its name.

In her green-and-raspberry dining-room, furnished in Chippendale style, Agnes Gemmell serves only breakfast, but the Anchorage Inn by the harbour, which has an ambitious menu, is a walk across the fields or a short drive away. Near it is Dunure Castle, a ruin now but with a better preserved dovecote. Here, in a dispute over land, an unfortunate was roasted alive by an Earl of Cassilis.

A couple of centuries later, a more civilised Earl of Cassilis got Robert Adam to rebuild his castle at Culzean. Standing on a headland, Culzean was designed by Adam to take advantage of the seaward views which are so great a feature of this coast. Owned with its excellent park by the National Trust for Scotland, it is, with the area's many Burns associations, a big draw to Carrick, as this part of Ayrshire is known; though golfers may find nearby Turnberry more compelling.

EAGLESCAIRNIE MAINS
Gifford, East Lothian, EH41 4HN (Lothian)   Tel: 01620 810491
South of Haddington. Nearest main road: A1 from Haddington to Edinburgh.

rear view

3 Bedrooms. £16–£20 (less for 4 nights). Two have own bath/shower/toilet. Tea/coffee facilities. Views of garden, country. No smoking. Washing machine on request.
Dinner. £10 for 3 courses and coffee at times to suit guests. Non-residents not admitted. Vegetarian or special diets if ordered. Wine can be brought in. **Light suppers** if ordered.
1 Sitting-room. With open fire, central heating, TV.
Large garden.

The name tells you this was the main farm on an estate. In the 18th century (when the handsome farmhouse was built) the estate was run by a landowner who had made a fortune from cotton in Egypt.

The Williams family came here from Hampshire to farm – mainly sheep (lambing is in March), horses, game and wheat. They have won awards for their conservation work – planting hedges and 7000 trees, clearing ponds, providing wildlife notes for visitors, hosting courses on conservation for farmers, and so on (Michael runs the farm and does all this with only one helper). Around its borders are a river and streams, and adjoining it the lands of the Duke of Hamilton – Scotland's premier duke – to which Hess (who had met the then Duke at the Olympic Games) made his fateful flight.

Barbara Williams has decorated the sitting-room with coral moiré wallpaper and flowered chintz sofas by the log fire. Elegantly draped curtains frame the big, sash windows; there are antiques, watercolours and alcoves of china; and the Adam fireplace is carved with pastoral motifs – her grandmother acquired it from the family solicitor whose offices were in Edinburgh's celebrated Charlotte Square.

Most bedrooms enjoy two aspects (with views of the Lammermuir Hills) and have, for instance, peony-patterned fabrics and a fine bathroom. There's a pine breakfast-room with haggis and potato scones on offer; and another snug little sitting-room leading to a polygonal conservatory, one wall smothered with a climbing geranium (sometimes it is used also for such light suppers as cucumber-and-mint soup, lasagne and summer pudding, made with home-grown produce). Seated in the conservatory, one can enjoy the scent of jasmine and the sight of spectacular sunsets. And there are a games room, hard tennis court and golf-net too.

One can spend one's time exploring all the region between Edinburgh (only 20 miles) and the Borders where there are great houses and abbeys to visit. The Lammermuir Hills are wild and unspoilt.

EARLSFIELD FARM
Kennethmont, Aberdeenshire, AB52 6YQ (Grampian)
Tel: 014643 473
South of Huntly. Nearest main road: A97 from Huntly to Ballater.

3 Bedrooms. £14. One has own shower/toilet. Tea/coffee facilities. Views of garden, country. No smoking. Washing machine on request.
Dinner (if ordered). £6 for 3 courses and coffee at 7pm. Non-residents not admitted. Vegetarian or special diets if ordered. Wine can be brought in. **Light suppers** if ordered.
1 Sitting-room. With open fire, central heating, TV, video, record-player.
Small garden.

Gazing out benignly from his frame over the fireplace, Earlsfield's most respected elder statesman oversees breakfast with an aloof approval worthy of a Duke of Gordon himself. This patriarch, however, was only 11 years old when the portrait was painted: he is a magnificent Blonde d'Aquitaine bull. Earlsfield is a mixed farm, raising suckler cows and sheep as well as arable crops, and visitors are welcome to look round.

Accommodation is homely: on the ground floor are a family room and shower-room; upstairs, next to the bathroom, a large bedroom looks out over farm buildings and fields. By arrangement, Fiona Grant serves such meals as home-made soup, pork chops with fresh vegetables, and apple tart or lemon meringue pie. Porridge is on offer for breakfast.

Like **Faich Hill** (see elsewhere), which is farmed by David's uncle, Earlsfield attracts the kind of guests for whom the pleasure of staying on a working farm in beautiful countryside outweighs the need for frills and fallals. Walkers come here for the Gordon Way; to the west, haunted Ballindalloch Castle opened to the public in 1994. Huntly Castle and the other houses of the Castle Trail are close, and the gardens of Leith Hall (NTS), a mile away, are open till dusk – a late hour in the summer at this latitude, making them an ideal focus for an evening stroll. Pony-trekking and hacking can be arranged at a nearby riding school.

Scotland's Castle Trail through Gordon district (Grampian region) takes in seven castles and two historic houses on a 150-mile signposted route, from Huntly Castle, begun in the 12th century, to the 18th-century Adam masterpiece Haddo House.

EASTER DALZIEL FARM C D
Dalcross, Inverness, IV1 2JL (Highland)   Tel: 01667 462213
East of Inverness. Nearest main road: A96 from Inverness to Nairn.

3 Bedrooms. £15–£17 (less for 2 nights). Tea/coffee facilities. Views of garden, country. Washing machine on request.
Dinner. £10 for 3 courses (with some choices) and coffee at 7.30pm. Non-residents not admitted. Vegetarian or special diets if ordered. Wine can be brought in. **Light suppers** if ordered.
1 Sitting-room. With open fire, central heating, TV, piano, record-player.
Large garden.
Closed from December to February.

Almost alone in Scotland, the inhabitants of Easter Dalziel pronounce its zed: Dalzeel not Deeyell.

Much of this charming farmhouse is at least 200 years old, though it was partially rebuilt in 1872. Margaret Pottie's father-in-law and husband have farmed here since the 1940s, raising beef cattle, sheep, and some arable crops. On the walls of the sitting-room hang paintings by Margaret's sister-in-law, who recently won a commission to supply paintings for ScotRail (to be displayed in first-class accommodation only!), as well as Margaret's own tapestries depicting farming subjects.

There are roses on the walls and fabrics in one bedroom, and more roses in the pretty green-and-pink, pine-panelled bathroom (there is another bathroom, with shower, downstairs). All the rooms have fine views over farmland and buildings, with woodland beyond, and the feeling is one of warmth and comfort, and being welcomed to the heart of a working farm. Dinner, served when farm commitments allow, reinforces this impression, since Margaret uses much of their own beef, lamb and vegetables when in season. Guests take breakfast together at the huge oak dining-table, with options that include porridge and kippers.

The Potties are happy to share their extensive knowledge of the area with guests, advising them on interesting trips and places to visit. Castle Stuart is only a mile away, and other popular destinations include Fort George, built on an isthmus in the Moray Firth after the '45, and now containing the museum of the Seaforth Highlanders, one of the regiments raised in the 18th century and amalgamated with the Cameron Highlanders in 1963. A new Jacobite Centre is due to open in Inverness in 1995, the 250th anniversary of the uprising led by Bonnie Prince Charlie; those with an interest in more distant history might prefer to see the impressive Clava and Ring cairns (NTS). Look out, too, for dolphins in the Moray Firth – one of only two schools in Britain (the other is in Cardigan Bay).

EASTER GLENTORE FARM
Greengairs, Lanarkshire, ML6 7TJ (Strathclyde)
Tel: 01236 830243
North of Airdrie. Nearest main road: A73 from Airdrie to Cumbernauld.

3 Bedrooms. £17–£25 (less for 4 nights). One has own shower/toilet. Tea/coffee facilities. Views of garden, country. No smoking. Washing machine on request.
Dinner. £10 for 3 courses and coffee at times to suit guests. Non-residents not admitted. Vegetarian or special diets if ordered. Wine can be brought in. **Light suppers** if ordered.
1 Sitting-room. With open fire, central heating, TV, piano, record-player.
Small garden.

On a quiet B road halfway between the villages of Greengairs and Slamannan, a sudden burst of colour dazzles one: a lovingly tended border, bright with antirrhinums, lobelias and petunias, which embraces the entrance to a neat farmyard flanked on three sides by low stone buildings. Swallows swoop under the eaves of the former byre, which now houses the comfortably furnished dining- and sitting-rooms; bedrooms are in the original farmhouse, built in 1705.

Views are magnificent – from the sitting-room one can see the Campsie Fells to the west, and on a fine day right across to the Ochils in the north, with the Wallace Monument at Stirling, 15 miles away as the crow flies, clearly visible.

Elsie Hunter serves such dinners as home-made soup, home-produced lamb or beef with three vegetables, and pavlova or apple pie. Options such as Lorne sausage (a locally made sliced beef sausage), black pudding and haggis may be available for breakfast.

The farm is ideally situated for those who wish to take a break on the long journey north, but it deserves consideration as a holiday base too, since Stirling, Edinburgh and Glasgow are all within half-an-hour's drive, as is the 200-year-old conservation village of New Lanark, where social reformer Robert Owen (1771–1858) laboured to improve the lot of the workers at his father-in-law's cotton mills. Today, visitors to the centre can experience the sights and sounds of another century in this 'world heritage village'; the Summerlee Heritage Trust at Coatbridge and the Weavers' Cottages Museum at Airdrie are also reminders of the area's rich industrial heritage.

Closer still are the Fannyside Lochs, where international windsurfing championships are held. The Forth and Clyde Canal, first opened in 1790, is undergoing restoration a few miles away. And all around is lovely countryside in which it is easy to forget one is so close to some of the principal cities of Scotland.

EDENSIDE HOUSE D M PT
Edenside, St Andrews, Fife, KY16 9SQ Tel: 01334 838108
North-west of St Andrews. On A91 from St Andrews to Cupar.

9 Bedrooms. £20 (less for 6 nights). Prices go up at Easter. All have own shower/toilet. Tea/coffee facilities. TV. Views of garden, country, sea, river. No smoking.
Light suppers if ordered.
1 Sitting-room. With open fire, central heating. No smoking.
Small garden.
Closed from December to February.

Not strictly off the beaten track, Edenside House is nevertheless perched right on the shore of the Eden Estuary Nature Reserve, a Site of Special Scientific Interest which supports one of the highest densities of birdlife in Britain. Serious birdwatchers come here in winter – among other rarities is the most northerly wintering flock of black-tailed godwits – but even the less dedicated can enjoy the waders and divers, grebe, shelduck and eider, and the occasional seal or porpoise, to be seen in the area.

On entering the modernised 18th-century farmhouse one steps straight into the comfortable sitting-room, with open-tread staircase leading up to three bedrooms above. The blue room, with windows on two sides, is particularly attractive. The dining-room is furnished with pine, and there are comfortable cane chairs in all the pretty, fresh-looking rooms in the single-storey annexe, several of which overlook the estuary.

Jim and Margaret Mansell ran a licensed hotel before coming to Edenside. However, they found they had no time to be with their guests, which they discovered was what they liked best about the business, so they decided to leave the hotel and come here. They serve light suppers only, but St Andrews with its wide variety of eating-places is only five minutes away. The breakfast menu includes porridge, mushrooms on toast and smoked haddock as well as more familiar options.

St Andrews' famous golf links are between Edenside and the city, and the local bus stops right outside the gate. Sixteenth-century Earlshall Castle with its magnificent gardens is near; Mary Queen of Scots visited it in 1561 and her bedchamber with period furnishings is open to the public. Across the estuary, Tentsmuir Forest attracts walkers, and St Andrews itself, home of Scotland's oldest university (founded in 1412) and with a splendid cathedral as well as the castle, is worth a prolonged visit.

ENRICK COTTAGE
Drumnadrochit, Inverness, IV3 6TZ (Highland)
Tel: 01456 450423
South-west of Inverness. On A831 from Drumnadrochit to Cannich.

2 Bedrooms. £14–£16. Prices go up in July. Both have own bath/shower/toilet. Tea/coffee facilities. Views of garden, country, river. No smoking.
Light suppers sometimes.
1 Sitting-room. With central heating, TV. No smoking.
Small garden.
Closed from November to February.

A long-ago copying error has left a legacy of confusion at this white-painted cottage: Enrick or Enrich? Logic and the Rapers suggest it was named for the River Enrick which flows a few yards from the bottom of the garden, but at some point an h was substituted for the k and now a splendid ambiguity prevails. Letters and inquirers for either, however, are directed to the same pretty cottage, whose back is visible from a major road but which faces south across the tranquil river to Glenurquhart Forest beyond.

This is the view from the bedrooms, both of which are at the front of the house. Sunny colour schemes and bright fabrics complement Alan's furniture, and since neither room is large the provision of a deep window-seat in one of them (there is a sofa in the other) is an excellent use of space. All the paintings and tapestries on the walls are by Avis or her friends, and an antique table on the landing carries a wide selection of leaflets about local attractions.

Downstairs, more of Alan's furniture fills the sitting/dining-room. Don't be surprised if you are asked to try one of the chairs for size, for Alan makes them on a commercial basis and is fascinated by the different requirements of different bodies. Occasionally, by arrangement only, he runs wood-turning courses for guests.

There are no sausages or fried eggs for breakfast here. Instead, you might be offered a hot platter of scrambled eggs, bacon and tomatoes or fresh fruit, peeled and sliced; and freshly squeezed orange juice. Avis serves light suppers only, but guests can eat well and variously in Drumnadrochit (the name means 'the bridge on the ridge'), half-a-mile away.

Don't miss lovely Urquhart Castle on the shore of Loch Ness, surely recognisable from its photograph in any self-respecting Scottish calendar; or the rival Loch Ness Monster exhibition centres in Drumnadrochit.

ERICSTANE FARM
Moffat, Dumfriesshire, DG10 9LT (Dumfries & Galloway)
Tel: 01683 20127
Nearest main road: A701 from Dumfries to Edinburgh.

2 Bedrooms. £15 (less for 4 nights). Both have own bath/shower/toilet. Tea/coffee facilities. TV. Views of garden, country, river. Washing machine on request.
1 Sitting-room. With wood-burning stove, central heating.
Large garden.

When *Farmer's Weekly* published an article about role reversal based on Ericstane – where Robert Jackson looks after the bed-and-breakfast guests while Jane manages the stock – the result was a flood of visitors to the Annan Valley and this 800-acre hill farm, whose name means a place of atonement.

The house was semi-derelict when the Jacksons came here in 1988, a sad decline from its heyday before the First World War when five gardeners were employed in the grounds alone – you can still see the remains of the old kitchen garden, as well as a clump of dogtooth violets in the very spot where they flourished a century ago. The dining-room window frames a view of a fine cut-leaved beech.

Robert and Jane have refurbished the house to something like its former glory, restoring the front to its original Georgian elegance, and filling the rooms with antique furniture and lots of books. A 17th-century court cupboard divides sitting- and dining-areas; guests take breakfast at two fine elm gateleg tables.

One huge bedroom has a built-in cupboard with doors made by Robert from window shutters, a wooden bed with blue-and-white covers, and a big, light-filled shower-room. All the doors, skirtings and banisters have been lovingly stripped.

At breakfast, guests help themselves to bacon, eggs and sausages; Robert always has porridge on the go as well. He doesn't serve dinner, but there is a good variety of eating-places in Moffat, four miles away.

The scenery here is dominated by the dramatic Devil's Beef Tub, a vast natural hollow flanked by steeply rising hills. On one, Ericstane Brae, a gold brooch dating from 300 AD was found in the late 1800s on the Roman road which crosses it.

Most people come here to walk, for the countryside is spectacular; fishing and birdwatching are popular too.

53 ESKSIDE WEST
Musselburgh, Midlothian, EH21 6RB (Lothian)
Tel: 0131-665 2875

C(10) **PT S X**

Nearest main road: A199 from Edinburgh to Musselburgh (and A1 from south).

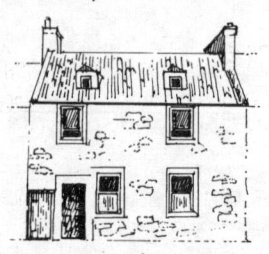

2 **Bedrooms.** £15–£18 (less for continental breakfast). Prices go up in June. Both have own bath/shower/toilet. Tea/coffee facilities. TV. Views of garden, country, river. No smoking. Washing machine on request.
Dinner. Up to £15 for 3 courses and coffee at times to suit guests. Non-residents not admitted. Vegetarian or special diets if ordered. Wine can be brought in. **Light suppers** if ordered.
1 **Sitting-room.** With open fire, central heating, TV, record-player.

No longer a fishing harbour, Musselburgh – nicknamed 'the honest town' – is now almost a suburb of Edinburgh (the centre is only about 10 minutes away by bus or rail). It has, too, its own attractions: grassy-banked River Esk – frequented by swans as well as trout and salmon – flows into the Firth of Forth through the middle of the town; there is a theatre-in-the-round that puts on good plays and ballet; and a fine old church, ancient tolbooth, and year-round horseracing. It also has the oldest golf course in the world, with others nearby.

Annie Deacon lives in what was a fisherman's cottage two centuries ago, on the bank of the river where almond and cherry trees flower in spring. A perfectionist, she redecorates rooms every year so that they always have a fresh look. White walls and lace spreads complement wildflower fabrics and bedheads. She makes much use of simple coir matting, bamboo furniture and pine-boarded walls, which are admirably suited to the simple house. Her home is full of books, paintings, pot-plants and flowers.

Annie was previously a professional caterer, producing businessmen's lunches, and she now brings her skills to bear upon the dinners which attract so many visitors back to stay again and again. She uses much local fish and game, cooking pheasant with gin and juniper berries, for instance, or roasting venison in oatmeal – accompanied by up to five vegetables (dressed with herbs) from her garden. A glass of wine is included in the price. And for breakfast you may be offered sausages she has smoked herself, or scrambled eggs with smoked salmon.

She is a good adviser on shopping for traditional Scottish produce to take home – cheeses, shortbread, whisky and liqueurs, haggis, kippers, smoked salmon or oatcakes. (Not to mention tweed, tartans and cashmere; Edinburgh is also a mecca for collectors of antiques and books.)

Musselburgh is not merely a base from which to visit Edinburgh. Eastward lies a varied coastline with fine beaches and rugged cliffs.

FAICH HILL FARM
Gartly, Huntly, Aberdeenshire, AB54 4RR (Grampian)
Tel: 0146688 240
South of Huntly. Nearest main road: A97 from Huntly to Ballater.

2 Bedrooms. £16. Both have own bath/shower/toilet. Tea/coffee facilities. Views of garden, country. No smoking.
Dinner. £9 for 3 courses and coffee at 6.30pm. Non-residents not admitted. Vegetarian or special diets if ordered. Wine can be brought in. No smoking.
Light suppers if ordered.
2 Sitting-rooms. With central heating, TV, record-player. Piano. Smoking in sunroom only.
Small garden.

Margaret Grant is too modest to draw guests' attention to the photograph on the piano in the dining-room, but is happy to explain if they notice it. It shows her with Keith Floyd at Dillons bookshop in Aberdeen, where he was promoting *American Pie* in 1989. That year, Faich Hill had won the Scottish Farmhouse of the Year award for the second time running, so Margaret was a natural choice when the Grampian Initiative Board wanted ambassadors to help persuade the television cook to write *Floyd in Scotland*. Fingers are still crossed at Faich Hill that they succeeded.

The great man himself could hardly better Margaret's menus for Scottish farmhouse fare: a starter of cockaleekie soup (chicken and leeks) or cullen skink (a traditional soup of smoked haddock, onions and potatoes, made with milk instead of stock) might be followed by pork-and-apple roulade, beefsteak pie or local salmon with vegetables from the garden, rounded off with a 'harvest pudding' of dried fruits, or Scotch trifle, made with whisky instead of sherry. Breakfast options include prunes, rhubarb and porridge.

The farmhouse itself is over 200 years old, and Theo's family has farmed here since 1884. In the bedrooms, brown velvet curtains match the bedheads and contrast with the pretty iris-patterned covers, while flamingoes march over the bathroom wallpaper nearby.

Many guests stay here for the walking – Tap o' Noth and Bennachie Hill are popular – but Huntly Castle (ancient seat of the Clan Gordon and once host to Robert Bruce) is well worth a visit, and the distilleries of the famous Whisky Trail are not far away. It was more than 500 years ago – in 1494 – that whisky was first distilled from barley, yeast and water.

FIORDHEM
Ord, Isle of Skye, IV44 8RN   Tel: 014715 226
Nearest main road: A581 from Broadford to Armadale.

3 Bedrooms. £32–£35 **including dinner.** All have own bath/shower/toilet. Tea/coffee facilities. Views of country, sea. No smoking.
Dinner. 3 courses and coffee at 7.30pm. Non-residents not admitted. Vegetarian or special diets if ordered. Wine can be brought in. No smoking.
Light suppers if ordered.
1 Sitting-room. With open fire, central heating, TV, video. No smoking.
Small garden.
Closed from November to February.

If you think the name sounds Swedish, you're right: this 'house on the fiord' was christened by Tony La Trobe's mother who emigrated to England in 1917. Tony's parents bought it as a ruined cottage in 1960 because it reminded his mother of Sweden, but she only holidayed here. It was left to Tony and Bridget to renovate it, practically from scratch, to the delightful place it is today.

Their energy and enthusiasm are infectious: guests compete hotly for the titles of Plucky Plodder, Path Pounder and Peak Performer on Tony's guided (or merely recommended) walks and climbs; then tuck in to one of Bridget's delicious dinners, which might be home-made vegetable soup or a haggis starter followed by venison braised in ale with orange and basil, or roast lamb with garlic and rosemary, and home-made apple or lemon meringue pie, or sticky toffee pudding.

The house is full of interesting items, all with stories attached: a splendid Victorian china foot-bath, an intricately carved Swedish sofa-bed, Staffordshire dogs on a solid old dresser in an alcove in the sitting-room, Bridget's collection of blue-and-white plates over the open fire. All the bedrooms have fresh, pretty fabrics and at least one fine old chair, and there are pictures and books everywhere. The best bedroom has huge picture windows overlooking Loch Eishort and Blaven (Bla Bheinn on some maps), at over 3000 feet not dwarfed even by the Cuillin Hills behind.

Otters play on the water's edge, 20 feet from the house; golden eagles nest in the glen. Alexander Smith wrote *A Summer in Skye* while staying at Ord in 1865. For further information, apply to Bridget and Tony: you couldn't hope for friendlier or more helpful hosts.

FLOWERBANK C D PT
Cree Bridge, Minnigaff, Newton Stewart, Wigtownshire,
DG8 6PJ (Dumfries & Galloway)   Tel: 01671 402629
Nearest main road: A75 from Dumfries to Stranraer.

7 Bedrooms. £15–£16 (less for 8 nights). Tea/coffee facilities. Views of garden, country, river. No smoking. Washing machine on request.
Dinner. £7.50 for 3 courses and coffee at 6.30pm. Non-residents not admitted. Vegetarian or special diets if ordered. Wine can be brought in. No smoking.
Light suppers if ordered.
1 Sitting-room. With open fire, central heating, TV.
Large garden.
Closed in December and January.

The young Edgar Allan Poe stayed in this house (now a listed building), then owned by a distant relative, in 1815; he was schooled in Great Britain. When Geoff and Linda Inker unblocked a long-closed room, they were disappointed to find nothing more gruesome than dust! The house was quite new when Poe stayed, but over the years it became neglected and, since they migrated here from London, the Inkers have worked hard to turn it once more into a comfortable place to stay.

Minnigaff, once bigger than Newton Stewart, is now almost a suburb of that town, just over the Cree Bridge. The Cree runs alongside the big garden of Flowerbank, and salmon are sometimes to be seen leaping in the river. The garden, with a hen-run at one end, supplies the kitchen, where Linda produces such entirely home-made meals as egg mayonnaise, beef crumble, and strawberry mousse; or lettuce soup, trout with croquette potatoes, and apple pie. The sitting-room, with its ceiling-high umbrella plant, overlooks the garden, as do most of the bedrooms, some giving views of the river.

Newton Stewart is a lively place, with a good museum and a mohair mill you can visit (a few miles away, you can also have a conducted tour of Scotland's most southerly distillery). There are close associations with Burns and Scott, and it was at Newton Stewart station, now closed, that Richard Hannay began his flight into the hills in *The Thirty-nine Steps*.

To the south is Whithorn, where the 12th-century priory ruins are on the oldest Christian site in Scotland; even older remains are being excavated. Readers of *Ring of Bright Water* may know of this area as the home country of Gavin Maxwell, an ancestor of whom built Port William in 1770 as the first holiday village in Scotland.

FORESTERS HOUSE   C D X

Newton, Moray, IV30 3XW (Grampian)   Tel: 01343 552862
West of Elgin. Nearest main road: A96 from Inverness to Aberdeen.

2 Bedrooms. £14–£16 (less for 7 nights). Both have own toilet. Views of garden, country. No smoking. Washing machine on request.
Light suppers if ordered.
1 Sitting-room. With open fire, central heating, TV, record-player.
Garden.

The influence of the Forestry Commission is still clearly evident at Foresters House – not only in the name (it really was the head forester's house until the Commission sold it to the Goodwins) but also in the sound of the hooter which summons forestry workers to their posts at 8am. Triple-glazing in the two light and airy bedrooms ensures that guests who do not have to answer the call are left undisturbed! Both rooms are large enough to take families; the green room with windows on two sides is particularly appealing.

Jennifer serves light suppers only, but breakfast choices are wide, including porridge, black pudding, naturally smoked kippers, herring, and tattie (potato) scones.

Within easy reach of Inverness and even Aberdeen, as well as the celebrated Whisky Trail, the area has much to commend it in its own right: the Speyside Way for walkers; Brodie, Cawdor and Kilravock castles; Elgin (cathedral, museum) and Forres; the coastal villages of Burghead and Findhorn (famous for its spiritual community); and, at Fochabers, the Baxter Visitors Centre, where you can tour the famous food factory and buy unusual specialities.

Sitting-room at Upper Woodinch, see p.123

THE GALLOWAY
22 Dean Park Crescent, Edinburgh, EH4 1PH
Tel: 0131-332 3672

10 Bedrooms. £17–£20 (less for 7 nights). Prices go up in April. Bargain breaks. Some have own bath/shower/toilet. Tea/coffee facilities. TV. Views of garden, city.
Dinner. £20 for 5 courses and coffee at 6.30–7pm. Non-residents not admitted. Vegetarian or special diets if ordered. Wine can be brought in.
1 Sitting-room. With central heating.
Small garden.

Dean still retains its own identity as a village within the city centre, even though buses whisk you to Princes Street and all the principal sights within five minutes. The 'New Town' planners began to develop a then rural area only in 1814, starting with picturesque Ann Street on a wooded cliffside site, the Water of Leith flowing below.

A 20-acre park on the river banks is exclusive to local residents, but if you stay at The Galloway Bob Clark will lend you a key to it: you can then walk among the trees from Ann Street to Telford's Dean Bridge, beyond which lie famous Charlotte Square (designed by Adam; one of its houses, owned by the National Trust for Scotland, can be visited) and Princes Street. Or, in the other direction, you can follow the Water of Leith all the way down to the harbourside on the Firth of Forth.

The Galloway is one of many terrace houses built around Dean Park for Victorian merchants. As with so many Edinburgh homes, the best cityscape views are from bedrooms on the second floor: from some you can even see, beyond the dramatic turrets of Fettes College and encircling hills, as far as Fife. Rooms vary but most are spacious: no. 3, for instance, which has a huge bay window and pretty plasterwork ceiling (originally it was the principal sitting-room of the house). Some have bathrooms with oval baths; one, with attractive patchwork bedspreads, a power-shower.

Dinner here (to be booked in advance) is something of an event. Pâté or soup will be followed by, for example, sole in cheese sauce; the main course often includes venison, partridge or other game; and after a gâteau or similar pudding come cheeses. (Alternatively, there are Edinburgh's many restaurants to sample – scores of them, of every nationality, and quite a number serving specifically Scottish dishes.) Breakfasts, too, are memorable for the choices offered, from ten kinds of cereal plus raspberries or other fruit to such options as white or black pudding, kippers with scrambled egg, a spicy fruit dumpling, or even, for the really robust, haggis.

The Galloway is well placed for visiting the Royal Botanic Garden (founded in 1680), Zoo and Gallery of Modern Art.

GLEBE HOUSE
Law Road, North Berwick, East Lothian, EH39 4PL (Lothian)
Tel: 01620 892608
Nearest main road: A198 from North Berwick towards Dunbar.

4 Bedrooms. £15–£18. One has own bath/shower/toilet. Tea/coffee facilities. Views of garden, sea. Washing machine on request.
Light suppers if ordered.
1 Sitting-room. With open fire, central heating, TV, piano, record-player.
Large garden.

The house now inhabited by the young Scott family was until recently a manse (vicarage), built in 1780, on the outskirts of this historic little town by the sea.

There is a huge dining-room with mahogany table and fiddleback chairs, rose chintz curtains and big sofas in the sitting-room, which has oil paintings and antiques too. One ground-floor bedroom is particularly pretty, having duvets in pale pink with white broderie anglaise and a carpeted bathroom (elegantly draped curtains in both). From others upstairs (via a landing lined with Breton pottery) there are views of Craigleith Island in the Firth of Forth or (beyond the garden and a field of sheep) strange Law Hill with a whalebone arch on its summit – a well-known viewpoint.

As there are so many excellent restaurants in North Berwick, Gwen does only light suppers.

The town is well placed for visiting Edinburgh (½ hour by car or train), Aberlady bird sanctuary, Dunbar's country park, the Lammermuir Hills (splendid walks), Dirleton Castle and many other sights. Mr Marr, who has the looks of a Viking, will take you out to the Bass Rock to spot seabirds and you can land on Fidra, haunt of seals – the original of Robert Louis Stevenson's *Treasure Island*. There are an ancient watermill at East Linton, many excellent beaches nearby, and at the fishing village of Eyemouth an award-winning museum that includes an actual cottage kitchen among its exhibits of local life and work.

John Muir (who emigrated to America in 1849 and founded its national parks) is commemorated by a fine, 2000-acre country park on the coast near Dunbar where his birthplace is open to the public. This historic region is a good one in which to bicycle (a leaflet of routes is obtainable at Tourist Information Centres), play golf, buy crafts, and discover the many picturesque villages and outstanding churches.

GLEBE HOUSE CDS
Terregles, Dumfries, DG2 9RR (Dumfries & Galloway)
Tel: 01387 720259
West of Dumfries. Nearest main road: A75 from Dumfries to Stranraer.

3 Bedrooms. £25 **including dinner** (less for 7 nights). Bargain breaks. TV. Views of garden, country. Washing machine on request.
Dinner. 4 courses (with some choices) and coffee at times to suit guests. Vegetarian or special diets if ordered. Wine can be brought in. **Light suppers** if ordered.
1 Sitting-room. With open fire, central heating, TV, piano.
Large garden.

There are no wall-to-wall antiques at Glebe House, nor carpets too precious to walk on: instead, an old grand piano with pianola action stands beside a somewhat eclectic collection of comfortable-looking sofas and chairs grouped round the log fire in the high-ceilinged sitting-room, with its pale green walls, red carpet and curtains, and white-painted shutters. When Joan Bailey bought the pianola (and 300 music rolls) she had actually gone out to look for a kitchen table, but she doesn't regret the impulse. Between them, she and her two daughters play the piano, clarinet, flute, guitar and drums, and sometimes, when the girls are at home and guests amenable, there is impromptu music-making after dinner.

The meal, though, is undoubtedly the main event of the evening. Joan is an outstanding cook, and guests are hard put to it to choose starters and puddings from such options as creamy egg-and-sorrel mousse or spiced mushroom pancakes; apple, date and coconut meringue pudding or one of Joan's home-made liqueur ice creams. There is no choice of main course, which might be chicken in a wine, grape and cream sauce, or sirloin bordelaise, served with imaginatively prepared vegetables. The breakfast menu is extensive, including devilled kidneys and haddock-and-salmon fishcakes; bread is home-made.

Glebe House was built in the 18th century as a Church of Scotland manse (some of the ministers who later lived here have returned as bed-and-breakfast guests), and although the sitting-room and kitchen are Victorian additions the bedrooms are in the original Georgian part of the house. The walls are hung with unusual samples of needlework: Joan, a former journalist, worked at one time on a series of specialist craft books, and was, she admits ruefully, the first person in Britain to write about the revival of macramé. She is the most delightful host anyone could wish for.

Although apparently deep in the countryside, Glebe House is only ten minutes from Dumfries town centre.

GLENDRISSAIG C
by Girvan, Ayrshire, KA26 0HJ (Strathclyde)   Tel: 01465 4631
South of Girvan. Off A714 from Girvan to Newton Stewart.

3 Bedrooms. £18–£22. **10% discount to readers of this book.** Two have own bath/shower/toilet. Views of garden, country, sea. Balcony. No smoking.
Dinner. £9 for 3 courses and coffee at 7pm. Non-residents not admitted. Vegetarian or special diets if ordered. Wine can be brought in. No smoking.
1 Sitting-room. With open fire, central heating, TV. No smoking.
Large garden.
Closed from November to March.

One of the things which first attracted Kate and Findlay McIntosh to Glendrissaig was its garden, designed by the landscape gardener who built the house in 1978 and still, thanks to the hard work of Findlay and Kate, a sheer delight. Productive, too: the McIntoshes' guests benefit from the organically grown vegetables, not to mention the 40 blackcurrant bushes.

Not surprisingly, the emphasis in the kitchen is on good, wholefood cooking (vegetarians actively encouraged); soups are home-made, as is the blackcurrant cheesecake (from those 40 bushes), and salads are plentiful. Meals are taken in the sitting/dining-room, painted in shades of coffee and cream, where guests eat at a table set at the window, and relax afterwards in the comfortable Ercol sofa and chairs.

Since the house is built on rising ground, even the pink ground-floor bedroom has stunning views west over the Firth of Clyde to Arran and the Mull of Kintyre (sunsets can be breathtaking), as well as to Byne Hill inland. Upstairs, a pine-furnished room with pale green walls and lilac ceiling looks out over the vegetable garden to Laggan Hill, another lovely prospect. The family room has rose-patterned paper and a cinnamon carpet; there are more roses in its pretty bathroom, and William Morris upholstery on a well-stuffed armchair.

Bathrooms here are of a very high standard, since Findlay runs a plumbing business; and it is particularly gratifying that Glendrissaig's private water supply is the only one in the area to fulfil all EU regulations – thanks, Findlay says, to a borehole 200 feet deep.

Walkers and birdwatchers come here for beautiful Glen Trool; the Southern Upland Way crosses the Galloway Forest Park via the glen, but there are innumerable shorter forest walks to enjoy as well. Up the coast are Culzean Castle and sandy beaches, and Girvan is midway between ferries to Arran (Ardrossan) and Northern Ireland (Stranraer).

GLENMARKIE FARMHOUSE C D M S
Glenisla, Perthshire, PH11 8QB (Tayside)   Tel: 01575 582341
North of Blairgowrie. Nearest main road: A93 from Blairgowrie to Aberdeen.

3 Bedrooms. £16. One has own bath/shower/toilet. Views of garden, country, forestry. No smoking. Washing machine on request.
Dinner. £11.50 for 3 courses and coffee at 7pm. Non-residents not admitted. Vegetarian or special diets if ordered. No smoking. **Light suppers** if ordered.
1 Sitting-room. With open fire, central heating, TV, video.
Small garden.
Closed in November.

At the end of three miles of very unbeaten track indeed, it is something of a relief as well as a pleasure to be welcomed by the Evanses' dogs and, shortly afterwards, by Sally and Simon themselves. The attractive turn-of-the-century farmhouse (originally servants' quarters for the nearby lodge) is set deep in Forestry Commission territory, and is probably the only bed-and-breakfast establishment in Scotland which actually sits on a cross-country ski trail – part of 40 miles of trails which attract many winter visitors. In addition, Sally takes riders of all abilities on escorted tours of the surrounding countryside; her qualification as a physiotherapist has occasionally proved exceedingly useful! Simon trained in hotel management at the Savoy; it is he who oversees the bed-and-breakfast while Sally is busy with the stables.

Upstairs are two rooms with dormer windows and pretty fabrics; the shared bathroom, like the rest of the house, is full of mementoes from other parts of the world. On the landing hang two colourful paintings of Scarborough – but this is Scarborough, Tobago, where Sally lived as a child, though her father's family came from this area and even boasts a local hero, her grandfather Preston Watson, who some believe may have flown before the Wright brothers.

Downstairs is another bedroom bright with roses and poppies, with en suite bathroom; in the sitting-room one sinks back into one of the all-embracing chairs and sofas and contemplates, perhaps, tomorrow's ride or tonight's dinner, which might comprise leek-and-tomato soup or melon with prawns; local lamb, fish or venison; and bread-and-butter pudding or raspberry pavlova. Breakfast options include porridge, smoked haddock and herbal tea; jam and marmalade are home-made, eggs from the Evanses' chickens.

For those who wish to do more than explore the surrounding area on foot, ski or horseback, the Evanses recommend trips to Braemar and Balmoral castles, Pitlochry and Kirriemuir (J. M. Barrie's birthplace).

GLENTEWING FARM
Crawfordjohn, Lanarkshire, ML12 6ST (Strathclyde)
Tel: 018644 221
South-west of Biggar. Nearest main road: A74 from Abington to M6 and Carlisle (and M74, junction 13).

2 Bedrooms. £14–£18 (less for 5 nights or continental breakfast). Both have own bath/shower/toilet. Tea/coffee facilities. TV. Views of garden, country, river. No smoking. Washing machine on request.
Dinner. £6 for 3 courses and coffee at 6.30–7.30pm. Non-residents not admitted. Vegetarian diets if ordered. Wine can be brought in. No smoking.
Light suppers if ordered.
1 Sitting-room. With central heating, TV. No smoking.
Garden.
Closed in December and January.

Margaret Hyslop is no stranger to bed-and-breakfast: she offered it in her previous farmhouse for 19 years before coming to Glentewing in 1993, when her husband John semi-retired from farming. Now they raise just a few sheep and beef cattle on land which, like **Netherton Farm** (see elsewhere), was once part of former prime minister Sir Alec Douglas-Home's estate.

The house, built at the turn of the century, is set in lovely countryside only a few miles from one of the most frequently used routes from England to Edinburgh and Glasgow, so is ideally placed for a stopover (and a day or two's rest) in one direction or the other. Views from all windows are of farmland and wooded hillside, and in the sitting-room there are deep blue leather chairs and sofa from which to enjoy them.

The bedrooms, at the front of the house, are large and immaculate, with pastel colour schemes; one has a very good blue-and-cream bathroom, the other a roomy shower. In the dining-room, with magnificent mahogany sideboard and table, Margaret serves traditional farmhouse dinners like home-made soup followed by the farm's own lamb, salmon or venison, with home-grown vegetables whenever possible. There might be bread-and-butter pudding or a steamed pudding to finish, and Margaret still boils her clootie dumpling in a cloth. For those who want to stretch their legs, there is a pub at Crawfordjohn which serves excellent bar food at very reasonable prices.

At breakfast, guests help themselves from a hot platter containing haggis and black pudding among other options; porridge is on offer too.

Only one hour from Dumfries, Glasgow and Edinburgh, Glentewing is an ideal base from which to tour southern Scotland. The Southern Upland Way crosses the Lowther Hills just to the south, and there is a Scottish Wildlife Trust visitor centre at the nearby Falls of Clyde.

GLENTOWER HOUSE   C D S
Glen Devon, by Dollar, Clackmannanshire, FK14 7JY (Tayside)
Tel: 01259 781282
South of Auchterarder. On A823 from Yetts of Muckart to Auchterarder.

5 Bedrooms. £17.50–£20. Some have own bath/shower/toilet. Views of garden, country, river. No smoking. Washing machine on request.
Dinner. From £12.50 for 3 courses (with choices) and coffee at times to suit guests. Vegetarian or special diets if ordered. Wine can be ordered. No smoking. **Light suppers** if ordered.
1 Sitting-room. With open fire, central heating, TV. Bar.
Large garden.

When, in 1982, fire ravaged a 40-bedroom hotel in lovely Glen Devon, Valerie Taylor's father, a surveyor, came to inspect the damage with a view to converting the property into flats. Instead, he recognised an opportunity to restore a fine old Victorian country house to its former splendour, and the result is Glentower, for ten years Valerie's family home and now a delightful guest-house and restaurant. Valerie has spent some time researching the history of the place, back through its days as that doomed hotel to the factor's lodge built in 1880, and further still to the 'butt and ben' cottage of 1715, just four walls and a pitched roof.

The distinctive tower houses a wooden spiral stair whose central pillar is an old ship's mast. Some of the original Victorian stained glass can still be seen in doors and windows, but there is nothing old-fashioned about the bedrooms, which are light and pretty, with lots of pale green and white paint offset by damson trimmings, and glorious views of the Ochil Hills or the spectacular Devon gorge. Access to the bedrooms from the main part of the house is via the winding stair; for those less steady on their feet, there is a door at the other end of the corridor which opens onto the grounds (the house is built on a hillside).

Meals are served in the low-ceilinged dining-room, where more pale green paint contrasts with darkly stained wood, and one wall is lined with windows that afford a dizzying prospect of the River Devon, tumbling between steep wooded banks far below. Both Valerie and her husband have catering backgrounds, and Valerie is helped in the kitchen by her mother – Atholl Crescent trained – so the food is excellent: smoked trout salad or haggis and neeps to start, perhaps, with pork and apricots in a mustard sauce or spinach-stuffed chicken with a lemon-and-ginger sauce to follow, and clootie dumpling or bread-and-butter pudding to finish.

GLOAGBURN FARM   C PT S X
Tibbermore, Perth, PH1 1QL (Tayside)   Tel: 01738 840228
West of Perth. Nearest main road: A85 from Perth to Crieff (and A9 from Perth to Stirling).

3 Bedrooms. £18–£20 (less for 2 nights. One has own bath/shower/toilet. Views of garden, country. No smoking. Washing machine on request.
Dinner. £10 for 3 courses and coffee at times to suit guests. Non-residents not admitted. Vegetarian or special diets if ordered. Wine can be brought in. No smoking. **Light suppers** if ordered.
1 Sitting-room. With open fire, central heating, TV. No smoking.
Large garden.

The bedrooms in this traditional, homely farmhouse are all so attractive that to pick out one feature seems invidious, but everyone will be fascinated by the original Edwardian light fittings in two of them: ingenious contraptions which utilise weights and pulleys to enable the user to position the light at any height required. Particularly attractive is the room with old brass bedstead, blue-and-white loveknot curtains and a view of the Ochil Hills; but the room with wooden beds and rosy wallpaper, and the family room with sprigged fabrics, are very appealing too. There is a pink-and-green bathroom upstairs, and a blue-and-white shower-room downstairs which has a lovely old brass-framed mirror.

Ian Niven's family has farmed here since 1924; now he raises sheep, beef cattle, and barley (for whisky). By arrangement, Alison serves such dinners as home-made soup or pâté, steak pie or a hearty casserole, and a pudding which depends on the fruit season, but might be apple tart or crème brûlée. At breakfast you might be offered porridge served cold with yogurt, fresh fruit and muesli; and fish is usually on the menu. Eggs are fresh from the Nivens' own hens.

Gloagburn is an ideal base from which to explore Perth, Crieff and the surrounding area; Huntingtower Castle is near, and the village of Tibbermore itself has an unusual little church and peaceful graveyard which make a perfect focus for an evening stroll. Children enjoy riding the Nivens' pony, too.

Readers' comments: Bedrooms huge, comfortable and well furnished.

In Scotland, the region is not part of the postal address. It is included in the entries for map reference only.

GREENHILL
Hownam, Roxburghshire, TD5 8AW (Borders)
Tel: 01573 440505
East of Jedburgh. Nearest main road: A68 from Corbridge to Edinburgh.

4 Bedrooms. £16.50–£17. Views of garden, country. No smoking. Washing machine on request.
Dinner. £10 for 3 courses and coffee at 7pm. Non-residents not admitted. Vegetarian or special diets if ordered. Wine can be brought in. No smoking.
Light suppers if ordered.
1 Sitting-room. With open fire, TV.
Large garden.

The bathrooms at Greenhill are a source of mingled envy and delight to the Harrises' visitors, but opinion is divided over which is the more appealing: the deep, old-fashioned baths themselves or the instructive 'Please pull' printed on the china handles at the ends of the lavatory chains.

The bedrooms, too, retain the dignity natural to a shooting-lodge built for a duke – in this case, the Duke of Roxburgh – in the 1830s. Two are huge, with antique furniture, pretty fabrics and splendid views of the quite lovely countryside with which Greenhill, nestling at the foot of the Cheviots some three miles from the border, is surrounded.

Downstairs, there is a sitting-room with lots of comfortable, well-worn sofas and chairs, and a dining-room redolent with fresh flowers where dinner is served, by candlelight, on a white linen tablecloth. Julia enjoys cooking, and might produce home-made pâté or melon followed by roast pork or a casserole of beef in beer with four fresh vegetables, and home-made profiteroles or chocolate gâteau.

Its tumultuous history has ensured that there is much to do and see in this beautiful border country. Roughly equidistant from Kelso and Jedburgh, Greenhill is an easy drive from both, and guests can visit Mary Queen of Scots House and the abbey at Jedburgh, and, a few miles north, the Waterloo monument at Peniel Heugh, where the surrounding woods were planted in the formations of the opposing armies at the start of the battle. There are hill forts on Hownam Rings and Hownam Law. Worth exploring, too, are Floors Castle (where Prince Andrew proposed to Sarah Ferguson) and the ruins of Roxburgh Castle and the abbey at Kelso – which Sir Walter Scott (who went to school here) called 'the most beautiful if not the most romantic town in Scotland'.

HARELAWSIDE FARM   C S
Grantshouse, Berwickshire, TD11 3RP (Borders)
Tel: 01361 850209
North-west of Berwick-upon-Tweed (Northumberland).
Off A1 from Berwick-upon-Tweed to Edinburgh.

4 Bedrooms. £15–£17 (less for 8 nights). Prices go up in May. One has own bath/toilet. Tea/coffee facilities. Views of garden, country, river. No smoking. Washing machine on request.
Dinner (by arrangement). £10 for 4 courses (with some choices) and coffee at 6.30–7pm. Non-residents not admitted. Wine can be brought in. No smoking.
Light suppers if ordered.
1 Sitting-room. With open fire, central heating, TV, piano, record-player. No smoking.
Garden.

There are indeed hares on the side of the hill ('law'); red squirrels and deer, too. And from the farm are outstanding valley views, with the Lammermuir Hills beyond, to be enjoyed from the dining-room tables.

Maureen Burton keeps the house spotless, and has used pale colours and very pretty fabrics in the bedrooms. She and her husband previously had a hotel (in Norfolk) so their standards are professional. He plays the church organ, as well as various instruments to be seen around the house (and sometimes heard, at breakfast-time).

The house is solid and handsome, with panelled doors and window-shutters, furnished appropriately with comfortable velvet armchairs and a log stove in the sitting-room – just the place in which to relax after one of Maureen's ample dinners (such as vegetable soup, baked local trout, raspberry trifle and cheeses), which she serves by arrangement only. She bakes her own bread.

Conveniently placed just off the A1, Harelawside is an arable and livestock farm (go in spring to see lambs and calves grazing naturally with their mothers – no 'factory farming' here) from which it is easy to explore the coast and its fishing villages in one direction and the hills in the other, Edinburgh to the north and the Borders to the south. The long Southern Upland Way ends at one of the sandy beaches near here, with dramatic St Abb's Head and its bird reserve further along. Apart from stately homes and museums, the region has beauty-spots to visit such as the hamlet of Abbey St Bathans and its trout farm in the hills, as well as fishing harbours (Dunbar has two – and a power station open to the public). In winter there are sheepdog trials to watch, ceilidhs and bagpiping, the Borders Festival (music, theatre, etc. throughout the region every October) and a spring River Tweed Festival in the Peebles area, and of course the superb autumn colours followed by snow on the spectacular hilltops.

HARTFELL HOUSE   D M S
Hartfell Crescent, Moffat, Dumfriesshire, DG10 9AL
(Dumfries & Galloway)   Tel: 01683 20153
Nearest main road: A701 from Dumfries to Edinburgh.

9 Bedrooms. £18–£22.50 (less for 8 nights). Prices go up at Easter. Five have own shower/toilet. Tea/coffee facilities. Views of garden, country.
Dinner. £10.50 for 3 courses (with choices) and coffee at 7pm. Non-residents not admitted. Vegetarian or special diets if ordered. Wine can be ordered. No smoking.
1 Sitting-room. With central heating, TV.
Large garden.
Closed from November to March.

Thanks to the new trunk road which now bypasses the town, Moffat can indeed lay claim to being 'off the beaten track', and Hartfell House, near the end of a quiet cul-de-sac and with its own terraced gardens stretching below it, is as secluded as the most exacting sleeper could wish. Built from local stone in 1850, the house reflects both general Victorian solidity and Moffat's particular prosperity at the time, when it was enjoying a prolonged period of popularity as a spa town.

Andrea and Alan Daniel came here from Windermere in 1989, and now run a comfortable and welcoming guest-house where the dining-room boasts doors and shutters of root oak stained, grained and gold-leaved with exquisite precision, a task which could have taken as long as six weeks per door. Meals are consonant with such a setting: a haggis and salad starter was delicious, as was the salmon steak with dill sauce; vegetables were perfectly cooked, and the blue Stilton was at its peak. Breakfast can include porridge or prunes; marmalade and raspberry jam are home-made.

It would be a mistake to dismiss Moffat as merely a stopover on the long journey between England and the more northerly parts of Scotland. The town is set among countryside which bears comparison with the most beautiful areas of northern England, if not the wilder grandeur of the Highlands, and is an ideal base for touring southern Scotland: Edinburgh, Glasgow and the east and west coasts are all within an hour's drive. For walkers, the Southern Uplands Way passes within a mile of the town. Close by, too, are the Devil's Beef Tub, the Grey Mare's Tail (NTS waterfall), St Mary's Loch, and Craigieburn, a frequent haunt of Robert Burns, who described his song 'Craigieburn Wood' as 'my favourite'.

HAWKCRAIG HOUSE C(8)
Aberdour, Fife, KY3 0TZ   Tel: 01383 860335
West of Burntisland. Nearest main road: A921 from Inverkeithing to Kirkcaldy (and M90, junction 1).

2 Bedrooms. £19. Prices go up in August and September. Both have own bath/shower/toilet. Tea/coffee on request. TV. Views of garden, country, sea, river. No smoking.
Dinner. £18.50 for 4 courses and coffee at times to suit guests. Vegetarian or special diets if ordered. Wine can be brought in. No smoking. **Light suppers** sometimes.
2 Sitting-rooms. With open fire, central heating, TV, record-player. No smoking.
Small garden.
Closed from November to mid-March.

The track leading to Hawkcraig House is not only unbeaten but practically vertical: not for the faint-hearted, the first experience of that short but almost sheer descent is truly hair-raising. Don't worry about the return ascent: Dougal Barrie is happy to walk ahead to ensure the coast is clear, and in extreme cases he will drive guests' cars up and down himself.

Once settled in the upstairs sitting-room with a soothing pre-dinner drink in hand, however, even the most agitated driver can hardly fail to be calmed by one of the most beautiful views in this book. The former ferryman's house, built in 1860, is perched right on the shore of the Firth of Forth, and one can see across the water to Edinburgh and the Pentland Hills. Nearer is the island of Inchcolm, with abbey, while in the foreground are sandy beaches and Aberdour village itself.

Dougal has knocked a window through from the dining-room to the sitting-room so that guests can enjoy the view even between courses of Elma's tempting dinners; a typical menu might be cream of watercress soup, goujons of local lemon sole, roast gigot of Scotch lamb with rosemary accompanied by four vegetables, and raspberry tart. When Elma was considering returning to science teaching after bringing up her family, her daughter's boyfriend said that after such a lapse she'd find her chemistry was only fit for cooking; Elma promptly decided to give up the teaching idea and go in for cookery. Now Hawkcraig House has earned Taste of Scotland recognition each year since 1982.

Both the sitting- and the dining-room are furnished with fine antiques; in the latter Elma's fondness for blue-and-white is reflected even in a pair of unusual Wedgwood-and-brass wall-mounted light fittings. Bedrooms are on the ground floor; one has a sea view, the other (with oval bath) looks over the garden. Breakfast is also served downstairs, and always begins with freshly squeezed orange juice.

HEATHBANK   C M PT
Boat of Garten, Inverness-shire, PH24 3BD (Highland)
Tel: 01479 831234
South-west of Grantown-on-Spey. Nearest main road: A95 from Aviemore to Grantown-on-Spey.

7 **Bedrooms.** £20–£30 (less for 8 nights). All have own bath/shower/toilet. Tea/coffee facilities. Views of garden, country. No smoking.
Dinner. £15 for 4 courses and coffee at 7pm. Vegetarian or special diets if ordered. Wine can be ordered. No smoking.
1 **Sitting-room.** With open fire, central heating, TV.
Large garden.
Closed from November to 25 December.

Boat of Garten is a peaceful little village and Heathbank is set well back from the road in its pleasantly unkempt garden, so it comes as something of a surprise – albeit a delightful one – when a full-sized steam train suddenly surges into view less than 100 yards from the sitting-room window. The Strathspey Steam Railway runs from Aviemore to Boat of Garten, and it is hoped to extend it northwards to Grantown-on-Spey as soon as funds permit.

The coming of the railway, in fact, was the reason for Heathbank's very existence: it was built around 1900 by the local postmaster as a boarding house for the visitors the new transport was expected to attract to the area. Lindsay and Graham Burge came here in 1988, and set about transforming Heathbank into something quite special.

Downstairs there is a private suite comprising a pink-and-dark-blue bedroom with cane chairs, an open fireplace and its own shower-room. Upstairs, a room decorated in grey and pink has a black-papered shower-room – the effect is dramatic. There is a four-poster in one room, while double peonies cluster over the ceiling of another. As befits a Victorian guest-house, most of the bedrooms are large enough to take a family; four have original cast-iron fireplaces. Particularly attractive is the blue shower-room set aside for users of a second-floor bedroom: the decoration includes a framed display of every blue-and-white stamp in Lindsay's collection. In one room, the bedhead is an inlaid panel from the front of an old piano.

Meals are cooked by Graham, a trained chef, using Scotch lamb, Spey salmon, or local pheasant, venison, trout, or beef; you might start with Orkney herring or home-made broccoli-and-hazelnut soup; pudding might be raspberry cranachan, an irresistible combination of fruit, whipped cream, toasted oatmeal, and sugar. You can always salve your conscience and waistline by going for the yogurt and fresh fruit option at breakfast.

HIGH BELLTREES FARM
Lochwinnoch, Renfrewshire, PA12 4JN (Strathclyde)
Tel: 01505 842376
South-west of Paisley. Nearest main road: A737 from Glasgow to Irvine.

5 Bedrooms. £15–£17 (less for 3 nights). Tea/coffee facilities. TV. Views of garden, country, loch (from one). Washing machine on request.
Light suppers if ordered.
1 Sitting-room. With open fire, central heating, TV, video.
Large garden.

It takes perhaps 20 minutes from the centre of Glasgow – 10 from the airport – to reach the turn-off to High Belltrees, yet this white-painted farmhouse, built in 1821, is set in rolling countryside with no hint of its proximity to one of Britain's principal cities. Views are of farmland and hillside, or towards the RSPB reserve at Lochwinnoch and Muirshiel Country Park beyond.

The three big, airy upstairs bedrooms, with their sloping ceilings, pastel colour schemes and pretty furnishings, share a green shower-room which enjoys the latter view; there is an attractive bathroom downstairs for the use of the two ground-floor bedrooms, and pictures are everywhere.

Breakfast is taken in the warm, comfortable sitting-room. Mary Mackie, a charming and helpful hostess, serves light suppers only and most guests dine at the Mossend Hotel, 1½ miles away.

Besides Glasgow, whose appeal as a tourist centre has grown steadily over the last few years, the area is rich in interest for the sightseer. Only a few miles from High Belltrees, the Weaver's Cottage at Kilbarchan houses the only remaining loom in a village which once boasted 800; you can watch a demonstration of weaving on it in the early 18th-century cottage.

The historic town of Paisley is overshadowed, literally and figuratively, by its larger neighbour Glasgow, but has much to offer on its own account: a magnificent abbey, parts of which date back to the 12th century; the world-famous collection of Paisley shawls in the museum; Sma' Shot Cottages (Victorian artisans' restored houses, with exhibition and loomshop); an arts centre in a converted 18th-century church; and much more.

Close to High Belltrees, fishers can enjoy a session of fly-fishing on the eight-acre loch at Howwood Trout Fishery. Southwards, at Ayr, is Robert Burns's cottage; and of course no one should miss the splendid Burrell Collection at Pollok Park, Glasgow, bequeathed to the city by nonagenarian shipping magnate William Burrell on his death in 1958.

HOPE COTTAGE C
Stenton, East Lothian, EH42 1TE (Lothian)   Tel: 01368 850293
South-west of Dunbar. Nearest main road: A1 from Dunbar to Edinburgh.

of garden, country. No smoking. Washing machine on request.
Dinner. £8.50 for 3 courses and coffee at times to suit guests. Non-residents not admitted. Vegetarian diets if ordered. Wine can be brought in. **Light suppers** if ordered.
1 Sitting-room. With open fire, central heating, TV.
Small garden.

2 Bedrooms. £18.50–£20.50 (less for 7 nights). Tea/coffee facilities. TV. Views

At the foot of the rolling Lammermuir Hills is hidden a conservation village with three greens, a pinnacled church, an old rood well, and a 'doocot' for 60 pigeons. On one green there still stands a tron for weighing fleeces, because once this was a weaving village.

At Hope Cottage Heather Allen gives her visitors an outstandingly warm welcome and the privacy of their own bathroom and little sitting-room (next to the ground-floor bedroom). Terracotta or book-lined walls are a cosy background to sofas beside the fire and the low table where Heather serves such meals as spinach soup, chicken in lemon and tarragon, chocolate mousse and cheese (a glass of wine is complimentary).

The cottage is full of character and has such individual touches as old cartoons of political bigwigs lining one wall, pretty Portuguese tiles in the downstairs bathroom, a terracotta-slabbed floor, fine oak table and beautifully carved newel-post in the kitchen/breakfast-room, and a vine-shaded conservatory overlooking the garden of roses and lavender. There are paintings everywhere, ladderback rush chairs, and a grandfather clock with a galleon pitching and tossing.

Stenton is near enough to London (4½ hours by rail) for short breaks from the south. There are excursion coaches from Dunbar, and a train that takes you into Edinburgh in ¼ hour.

There are five good (and cheap) golf courses in the vicinity, many Border mills where you can buy bargain woollies, Gullane's bird sanctuary, and lots of fishing villages – the auction at Eyemouth is an interesting spectacle. The Allens say their guests most enjoy the beautiful park and mansion of Lennoxlove, Thirlestone Castle (housing art treasures and the Border Life museum), Manderston (celebrated for its silver-plated staircase, marble dairy and brilliant terraced gardens), and vast Tantallon Castle, awesome on its rocky headland.

Readers' comments: Good value for money; excellent, substantial breakfasts; an exceptionally warm and courteous welcome from charming owners; friendly and attentive hosts.

THE HOUSE OF MARK
Invermark, Glenesk, Angus, DD9 7YZ (Tayside)
Tel: 01356 670315
North-west of Brechin. Nearest main road: A90 from Stonehaven to Forfar.

4 Bedrooms. £18 (less for 4 nights). Views of garden, country, river. No smoking. Washing machine on request.
Dinner. £10 for 3 courses and coffee at 7.30pm. Non-residents not admitted. Vegetarian or special diets if ordered. Wine can be brought in. No smoking.
Light suppers if ordered.
2 Sitting-rooms. With open fire, TV, piano, record-player. No smoking.
Large garden.

There is only one narrow, twisting, tree-lined road into Glenesk. For 15 miles, it takes you through some of the loveliest countryside in Angus before you come to Invermark and, literally, the end of the road. Here, at the mouth of Glen Mark, stands a former Church of Scotland manse, now part of the Dalhousie estate and home of Bea and Dick Rawlinson and their young family.

Flair and hard work have recreated a truly Victorian atmosphere from top to bottom of this three-storey house; the Rawlinsons' attention to detail extends even to the bolts on the lavatory door. The pink-and-blue downstairs bedroom has working shutters and an old-fashioned iron bedstead (painted, however, a delightful but distinctly un-Victorian pink). Two of the large, high-ceilinged bedrooms overlook the Water of Mark, a tributary of the North Esk.

In the kitchen, Bea makes much use of local produce: home-grown fruit and vegetables whenever possible, locally caught game almost always. Venison, pheasant, hare and rabbit appear in a variety of delicious guises, or you might be offered salmon baked in parsley, thyme, lemon juice and white wine, or lamb with anchovies and walnuts. The starter might be game or vegetable soup, the pudding, pear and cardamom pie or bananas in spiced orange sauce.

Dinner is served in the generously proportioned kitchen, and coffee, theoretically, taken in the lovely period sitting-room, with its huge mirror surmounted by a gilded frieze depicting an emperor's chariot, drawn by six lions and hovered over by attendant angels. More likely, though, you'll linger at the big Victorian dinner-table, apple in hand, talking about everything and nothing with Dick and Bea. They possess the happy knack of turning visitors into friends, and the pleasure of their company will be remembered by all their guests.

Readers' comments: Simply splendid. Absolutely charming couple, first-class home cooking.

INVERGLOY HOUSE
Spean Bridge, Inverness-shire, PH34 4DY (Highland)
Tel: 01397 712681
North-east of Fort William. Off A82 from Spean Bridge to Inverness.

3 Bedrooms. £16. Tea/coffee facilities. Views of garden, country, loch. No smoking.
Dinner. £9 for 3 courses and coffee at 7.30pm. Non-residents not admitted. No smoking.
1 Sitting-room. With central heating. No smoking.
50-acre wooded estate.

A jug of silken poppies set at the curve of the staircase provides a splash of colour among the most restful of pale greens; indeed the overwhelming impression of Invergloy House is of relaxed elegance, from the Bechstein piano in the sitting-room to the charm of the low-ceilinged bedrooms above. It used to be the coach-house and stables of a long-gone mansion belonging to a centenarian suffragette who employed six gardeners; the magnificent grounds still contain many fine specimen trees, and stretch down to a private shingle beach on the shore of Loch Lochy.

Margaret Cairns – a professional musician who also used to demonstrate flower-arranging – has filled the house with Edwardian furniture to set off the pale walls and white-painted beams. In one long bedroom (where twin beds are placed foot to foot) the pretty fabrics are printed with blue mecanopsis and red poppies; from another there is a breathtaking view down to the loch; a third has an equally delightful woodland prospect. All the rooms are twin-bedded, and guests share two attractive bathrooms. The pale green sitting-room looks out over the loch to the mountains beyond.

Round the big old table in the dining-room, Margaret serves such dinners as roast lamb with rosemary or pork chops with orange and ginger, accompanied by lightly cooked vegetables; rhubarb-and-ginger crunch or home-made meringues with fresh fruit and cream; and cheeses.

The Great Glen is the name given to the valley of lochs Lochy, Oich and Ness – all three linked by the Caledonian Canal to the sea loch Linnhe to the south-west and the Moray Firth to the north-east, so that there is a continuous waterway between Fort William and Inverness. Beautifully situated near the foot of the glen, Invergloy House is an ideal centre from which to explore westward to Mallaig and the Isle of Skye, or eastward to Aviemore and the Spey Valley. Ben Nevis and Glen Coe are near; for monster-spotters Loch Ness is only a short drive away.

INVERSNAID LODGE
Inversnaid, Aberfoyle, Stirlingshire, FK8 3TU (Central)
Tel: 01877 386254
North-west of Aberfoyle. Nearest main road: A821 from Aberfoyle to Callander.

8 Bedrooms. £20–£24 (less for 4 nights). Prices go up at Easter. All have own shower/toilet. Tea/coffee facilities. Views of garden, country, loch. No smoking. Washing machine on request.
Dinner. £12 for 3 courses and coffee at 7pm. Non-residents not admitted. Vegetarian or special diets if ordered. Wine can be ordered. No smoking. **Light suppers** if ordered.
1 Sitting-room. With open fire, central heating, piano, record-player. Bar.
Large garden.
Closed from November to February.

On a wooded hillside overlooking Loch Lomond, surrounded by its own 50-acre nature reserve, Inversnaid Lodge is utterly idyllic. Here André Goulancourt runs photography workshops (very occasionally, painting and birdwatching too) while Linda Middleton oversees the day-to-day running of the house, built around 1790 as a shooting-lodge for the Duke of Montrose and owned by the Montrose estate until the 1930s.

Decoration and furnishings are immaculate, with pink-striped wallpaper and a discreet pink carpet in the sitting-room, peach walls with white cornices in the dining-room. Both rooms have deep bay windows looking down to the loch and the hills beyond, and there are books everywhere, many on photography but covering a wide range of other subjects as well.

Up the imposing staircase are eight bedrooms (four of them singles) pretty with Laura Ashley papers and delicate fabrics. Views are spectacular; the rooms that look out over the azalea garden are at their best in May and June. And autumn colours can be breathtaking.

Breakfast options include porridge, fish, unsweetened muesli and a compote of stewed fruit; eggs are from Linda's chickens. By arrangement, she serves such dinners as home-made smoked mackerel pâté, local lamb or venison casserole, and 'Jean's Peach Thingy': peaches poached with cinnamon, then topped with Greek yogurt and brown sugar and grilled. Lots of fish and salads too.

A 1000-acre RSPB reserve adjoins Inversnaid's land, making this a mecca for birdwatchers; and the 92-mile West Highland Way between Glasgow and Fort William passes along the east shore of Loch Lomond only a few hundred yards from the house.

Readers' comments: Stunning service and care given to individual needs, a real haven of peace; words cannot do them justice.

INVERVAR LODGE   C M S X
Glen Lyon, Perthshire, PH15 2PL (Tayside)   Tel: 01887 877206 or 877223
West of Aberfeldy. Nearest main road: A827 from Killin to A9.

4 Bedrooms. £13 (less for 7 nights or continental breakfast). Prices go up in April. Bargain breaks. One has own bath/shower/toilet. Tea/coffee facilities. Views of garden, country. No smoking. Washing machine on request.
Dinner. £8.50 for 3 courses (with some choices) and coffee at times to suit guests. Non-residents not admitted. Vegetarian or special diets if ordered. Wine can be brought in. No smoking.
Light suppers if ordered.
1 Sitting-room. With log-burning stove, central heating, TV. No smoking.
Small garden.

Having pointed Stan's brother in the direction of **Blair View** (see elsewhere), Stan and Brenda Hardy finally found the house they were looking for. A handsome 19th-century hunting-lodge on the Glen Lyon estate, Invervar stands in splendid isolation above the River Lyon surrounded by glorious mountain scenery: indeed, you can bag four Munros from the gate.

The lodge is built on the expansive lines typical of Victorian Scottish country houses. High-ceilinged and elegantly proportioned, the sitting-room accommodates the dining-table without feeling in any way cramped, the polished wood floor and cream walls enhancing the atmosphere of lightness and space.

Up the stairs, pleasingly carpeted in pale green with walls to match, two large bedrooms (one green, the other pink, with hand-painted tiles adorning the original fireplace) share a modern grey bath and separate lavatory where scarlet mats add cheerful colour. Two slightly smaller rooms can be let as a family suite: pale green walls and curtains contrast with a chocolate carpet in one, while the private bathroom has a splendid, gryphon-footed tub.

Dinners are straightforward and plentiful, starting perhaps with home-made soup or pâté followed by chicken or steak, and finishing with a choice of jam roly-poly or fresh fruit salad.

Walking aside, this part of Perthshire has much to offer: watersports on Loch Tay and Loch Earn; fishing; golf at Aberfeldy.

Also at Aberfeldy, just over General Wade's bridge, is the Black Watch memorial. In 1667 Charles II issued a commission to the chiefs of the Highland clans to raise companies to keep the peace: 'to watch upon the braes', as he put it. This was the origin of the Highland Watch; six companies of the 'black watch', so called for their dark tartans, were gathered into one regiment of Royal Highlanders in 1739, and first mustered in May 1740 near the bridge.

KILDONAN LODGE   PT
27 Craigmillar Park, Edinburgh, EH16 5PE   Tel: 0131-667 2793
On A7 from Edinburgh to Carlisle.

10 Bedrooms. £18–£24 (less for 4 nights at weekends). Prices go up in June. Most have own bath/shower/toilet. Tea/coffee facilities. TV. No smoking. Washing machine on request.
Light suppers if ordered.
1 Sitting-room. With open fire, central heating. Bar.
Small garden.

From the outside, there's nothing very off-the-beaten-track about this handsome Victorian villa on one of the main roads into Edinburgh. Step into the parquet-floored hall, however, and your impression will change.

The house has original stained glass and moulded ceilings, but Maggie and Bruce Urquhart have brought the place up to an immaculate new standard. Walls and ceiling in the sitting-room (with 'honesty bar' and a display of trophies for skiing, skating and Scottish dancing) have been painted in shades of pink, with the ceiling rose and cornices picked out in white; brown velvet curtains and working shutters frame the windows, and a fine oak fireplace dominates one wall. The dining-room, too, is beautiful, with table linen echoing the peachy tones of the paintwork, handsome dining-chairs, and a parquet floor ideal for occasional ceilidhs.

There is one bedroom on the ground floor, and stairs lead down from the hall to four more built on a lower level at the back; all have subtly patterned fabrics and spacious shower-rooms. On the first floor are five similarly furnished bedrooms, only two of which have to share a shower; the rooms range in size from compact right up to no. 8, above the sitting-room and as large as it.

There are several restaurants within walking distance, and all the variety of the city centre only a short bus-ride away.

Kildonan Lodge was built in 1847, and remained a private house for over 120 years. Its name is probably connected with the village of Kildonan on the Helmsdale river, scene of the great Sutherland gold rush of 1868–9 and earlier 'cleared' by the infamous Countess of Sutherland; many of those evicted emigrated to the Red River district of Canada, naming their settlement New Kildonan (now part of Winnipeg).

Britain's largest stage is in the £20 million Edinburgh Festival Theatre, opened in 1994.

KILMUIR HOUSE
Kilmuir, Uig, Isle of Skye, IV51 9YN   Tel: 01470 542262
On A855 from Uig to Kilmaluag.

3 Bedrooms. £14–£15. TV (in one). Views of garden, country, sea. No smoking. Washing machine on request.
Dinner. £9.50 for 3 courses and coffee at 7pm. Non-residents not admitted. Vegetarian or special diets if ordered. Wine can be brought in. No smoking.
Light suppers if ordered.
2 Sitting-rooms. With open fire, central heating, TV, record-player. No smoking.
Walled garden.

Sunsets here can be breathtaking. The two upstairs bedrooms face west, and from the windows you look straight out over Loch Snizort and the Little Minch to the Western Isles and beyond, across the empty Atlantic towards the coast of Newfoundland. For Kilmuir House, a former Church of Scotland manse, is set high above the road almost at the northern tip of Skye, and its situation could scarcely form a greater contrast with the south of England, where Roy and Sally Phelps left their work (he in atomic energy, she as a local councillor) in the early 1980s in order to move up here. Their daughters, too, have thrown themselves into their new life, the elder becoming proficient enough on the clarsach, or Celtic harp, to outshine even her Scottish schoolfellows.

In such a position, it is no surprise that the feeling upstairs is all of air and space, to which the white-and-gilt furniture and light, flowery fabrics add their share. Downstairs, a back bedroom, once the minister's study, looks out on hilly countryside, and a second bathroom boasts the girls' collection of novelty soaps, frequently added to by guests.

The elegant family sitting-room, furnished with fine antiques and comfortable green velvet armchairs, is sometimes offered to visitors, but more often they linger in the sitting/dining-room, with its blue chintz and open fire, where they might enjoy such dinners as homemade soup, pork in barbecue sauce with green peppers, and the Phelpses' own garden rhubarb crumble.

It was near Kilmuir, on the shore close to Monkstat House, that Flora MacDonald landed with 'Betty Burke' in June 1746 after the immortal journey from Benbecula 'over the sea to Skye'. The disguised prince escaped, but Flora was later arrested and imprisoned for a time in the Tower of London. After her release she married and emigrated to North Carolina, but returned to Skye in 1779, where she remained for the rest of her life. She died in 1790, and was buried wrapped in a sheet from Bonnie Prince Charlie's bed. Her monument stands just up the road from Kilmuir.

KIRKBEAG
Kincraig, Inverness-shire, PH21 1ND (Highland)
Tel: 01540 651298

North-east of Kingussie. Nearest main road: A9 from Inverness to Perth.

2 Bedrooms. £14–£15. Prices go up in June. Views of garden, country. Washing machine on request.
Dinner. £10 for 2 or 3 courses and coffee at times to suit guests. Non-residents not admitted. Vegetarian or special diets if ordered. Wine can be brought in.
Light suppers if ordered.
1 Sitting-room. With central heating, TV, record-player.
Garden.

How many of us have looked at unused chapels in lovely parts of Britain and thought how satisfying it would be to buy one? John Paisley took the opportunity to do just that in 1975. At first he used the building just to work in, but after ten years he converted it into a family home (though retaining the workshop). Now he and Sheila welcome guests for bed-and-breakfast, and John runs, in addition, residential courses in wood-turning and carving, stone-cutting and polishing, and silver-working.

Kirkbeag was built for the Free Church of Scotland in 1851, but ceased to be used in 1933. It was soundly constructed, and even after 50 years of neglect John was able to incorporate many of its original features in his conversion: the sitting-room upstairs has arched windows, and a beam in one bedroom still carries the hook from which a paraffin lamp would have hung to illuminate the worshippers below. He made most of the furniture himself, including the beds and the open-tread spiral staircase; cork tiles and pine panelling characterise the bathroom and downstairs shower-room, and heating comes from a huge anthracite-burning stove in the kitchen. There are books everywhere, reflecting the Paisleys' interests: John's collection of local myths and legends, for instance, brings a new dimension to walking the old drove roads hereabouts. John himself has been a professional mountaineer in the area around Kirkbeag for 16 years, and is happy to discuss routes with climbers who come here because of its proximity to the Cairngorms.

Dinner is served by arrangement only, and might comprise a starter such as cream of celery soup or corn-on-the-cob with a creamy butter sauce; lasagne or roast chicken; and apple pie or raspberry sherry trifle.

KIRKGATE HOUSE
St Cyrus, Montrose, Angus, DD10 0BL (Grampian)
Tel: 01674 850301
North of Montrose (Tayside). Nearest main road: A92 from Aberdeen to Dundee.

3 Bedrooms. £16 (less for 6 nights). All have own shower. Tea/coffee facilities. Views of garden, country.
Light suppers if ordered.
1 Sitting-room. With central heating, TV.
Small garden.

Built in 1814 as a coaching inn, this listed building stands beside the village green, hard by the church (there are 600-year-old ruins behind the present building) and a few minutes' walk from two miles of clean sand, with salmon nets and smugglers' caves.

Lillian and James Cargill were brought up a few miles north of here, and are knowledgeable and enthusiastic guides to the area. They came to St Cyrus in 1989, and converted the stable block into what was to have been a recording studio; instead, the extension now houses three very attractive bedrooms, two with white paint and louvred pine, the third with blue carpet and walls of palest pink. There are pretty, lacy curtains and stencils on the walls; in one room is a lovely seven-foot American bedhead.

Lillian offers light suppers only since the St Cyrus Hotel serves excellent bar food.

Breakfast is taken in the cosy sitting/dining-room: porridge and, appropriately, Arbroath smokies might be on offer.

The attractions of this part of the east coast are too often overlooked. Dramatic Dunnottar Castle near Stonehaven was one of the sets used by Franco Zeffirelli in *Hamlet*, starring Mel Gibson and Glenn Close. Stonehaven itself, with its picturesque harbour and Tolbooth Museum, should not be missed; nor the RSPB reserve at Fowlsheugh, the largest seabird colony in mainland Britain. From 1651 to 1660 the Scottish crown jewels were hidden in Kinneff Old Church; inland, the Grassic Gibbon Centre at Arbuthnott (with pre-Reformation church) commemorates the life and work of the author of *A Scots Quair*. Further west is Fasque, home of the Gladstone family. St Cyrus itself has a National Nature Reserve, and the Scottish Wildlife Trust's flagship visitor centre is due to open in the Montrose Basin in 1995. Johnshaven and Gourdon (childhood homes of Lillian and James) are lively fishing villages, where the catch is still sold straight from the sea.

KIRKSIDE OF MIDDLEBIE C D(♀) S
Lockerbie, Dumfriesshire, DG11 3JW (Dumfries & Galloway)
Tel: 01576 300204
South-east of Lockerbie. Nearest main road: A74 from Abington to M6 and Carlisle.

2 Bedrooms. £19–£20. Tea/coffee facilities. Views of garden, country. Washing machine on request.
Dinner (by arrangement). £12 for 3 courses and coffee at 7.30pm. Non-residents not admitted. Vegetarian or special diets if ordered. Wine can be brought in. **Light suppers** if ordered.
1 Sitting-room. With open fire, central heating, TV.
Large garden.

'Kirkside of Middlebie' means just what it says: the house beside the church in Middlebie. Until the 1970s it was still a Church of Scotland manse, solidly built around 1870; now Jock and Rosemary Milne Home offer bed-and-breakfast to groups of two, three or four people who don't mind sharing a bathroom.

The principal bedroom, with a lovely view of the garden, has a magnificent patchwork quilt on the double bed. A third person travelling with the occupants of this room would have the use of a very pretty yellow single on the other side of the bathroom, another couple a larger room with windows on two sides affording far views of rolling countryside and farmland.

Down the stone staircase, the walls of the dining-room are hung with leaf-patterned paper around the open fireplace with Inigo Jones mantelpiece. Meals are taken at a mahogany table; there is a handsome sideboard in the white-painted alcove.

More paintings of and by the family hang in the sitting-room, where deep, comfortable sofas and chairs are drawn up round the log fire. As in the dining-room, tall windows look out onto the garden; both rooms breathe elegance, with their graceful proportions and quiet charm.

Dinner might be pâté or chilled consommé, sea trout or locally shot game served with vegetables from the garden, and a mousse of chocolate or fruit. On other nights, guests might dine in Lockerbie or Annan, or at a very good restaurant – the Courtyard – a mile and a half down the lane at Eaglesfield. Fresh fruit appears at breakfast, or fruit salad.

Ecclefechan, birthplace of Thomas Carlyle, is less than two miles away; the fastest road from Carlisle to Glasgow or Edinburgh is even closer.

Prices are per person in a double room at the beginning of the year.

KIRNAN C(5) D
Kilmichael Glen, Argyll, PA31 8QL (Strathclyde)
Tel: 01546 605217
North of Lochgilphead. Nearest main road: A816 from Oban to Lochgilphead.

3 Bedrooms. £16–£18. One has own bath/toilet. Tea/coffee facilities. Views of garden. No smoking.
Light suppers if ordered.
1 Sitting-room. With open fire, central heating, TV, piano.
Large garden.

The origins of Kirnan can be traced back to the 17th century, when it was a Campbell stronghold; in 1890 the house was extended to form a shooting-lodge, and in 1920 the owner laid out gardens which contemporary horticulturalists rated second only to Inverewe. Today, David and Margaret Bracey can still point out stone slabs from the original paths in their 12-acre garden, at its best in May and June when the rhododendrons and azaleas for which the west of Scotland is famous are in glorious bloom. There are two trout lochs, and fishing can be arranged on the Braceys' own 4-mile stretch of the River Add.

Bedrooms are delightful, with flowery papers and fabrics and lovely views over the garden: wisteria and rhododendrons just outside one window, the much-frequented bird-table close to another. There are splendid old-fashioned lavatories, and on the landing an old porcelain sink with brass taps overflowing with houseplants.

The breakfast-room has William Morris curtains and an open fire; Margaret serves light suppers only, recommending a number of local restaurants for anything from bar snacks to Cordon Bleu dinners. Her hobby is needlework, and she will do tapestries of guests' houses from photographs. David worked as an estate agent in Bristol until, after 35 years of fishing trips to Scotland, he realised his ambition to move up here for good.

They chose a beautiful area, steeped in ancient history: 4000-year-old cup-and-ring designs can be seen cut into rock faces at Kilmichael Glassary ('valley') and elsewhere, and the Iron Age hill fort of Dunadd became the residence of the kings of Dalriada in the 6th century.

Nearby Crinan Moss is a Site of Special Scientific Interest; and there are several outstanding gardens to visit.

LANGDALE HOUSE C D
Waterloo, Breakish, Isle of Skye, IV42 8QE Tel: 01471 822376
East of Broadford. Nearest main road: A850 from Kyleakin to Portree.

4 Bedrooms. £16–£18 (less for 5 nights). Some have own bath/shower/ toilet. Tea/coffee facilities. TV. Views of garden, country, sea. No smoking. **Dinner.** £14 for 3 courses and coffee at times to suit guests. Non-residents not admitted. Vegetarian or special diets if ordered. Wine can be ordered. No smoking.
1 Sitting-room. With central heating, TV, record-player. Bar.
Garden.

At the end of a No Through Road less than ten miles from the Kyle of Lochalsh crossing lies this purpose-built modern bungalow, Myra and Ian Macgregor's very professionally run guest-house. The comfortable sitting-room has been designed to take maximum advantage of the house's situation on the south of Broadford Bay, with windows on two sides overlooking the sea, where seals can often be spotted (a telescope has been set up at one window for this purpose).

Bedrooms are fresh and spotlessly clean, with blue-and-pink or blue-and-cream colour schemes, and shower-rooms warmly lined with pretty vinyl. In the cinnamon-carpeted dining-room, guests eat at a table set at the window, where they can look out over the sea and the hills of Skye to the Red Cuillin rising beyond.

Myra used to teach home economics in Glasgow, and Ian was a butcher, so meals are beautifully prepared from the best ingredients. A sample dinner might be home-made soup or dressed avocado, followed by boeuf bourguignon or grilled Skye salmon, then fresh fruit salad or home-made lemon meringue pie. Porridge and kippers are usually available for breakfast.

With the completion of the road bridge between Kyle of Lochalsh and Kyleakin something of the romance of a journey to Skye has been lost, but be there never so many road links between it and the mainland, the attractions of the island will never be diminished. The scenery is breathtaking, and no one who has seen the extraordinary, menacing and beautiful silhouette of the Cuillin Hills piercing a sunset sky will ever forget it. Neither the mountainous splendour of the north nor the milder woodland of the Sleat peninsula in the south should be ignored, or the seats of the two great rival clans of the island: Dunvegan Castle of clan Macleod in the north-west, and Armadale Castle of clan Donald in the south-east. Both have gardens which are open to the public, and the latter houses the Clan Donald Centre. There are croft museums, and at Carbost is Skye's only distillery, the great Talisker, Robert Louis Stevenson's 'king o' drinks'.

LAWHILL HOUSE   C D S
Trinity Gask, Perthshire, PH3 1LJ (Tayside)   Tel: 01764 683288
(messages: 0131-661 1889)
North of Auchterarder. Nearest main road: A9 from Perth to Stirling.

3 Bedrooms. £20 (less for 4 nights). Views of garden, country, river. No smoking. Washing machine on request.
Dinner. £12–£15 for 3 courses (with some choices) and coffee at times to suit guests. Non-residents not admitted. Vegetarian or special diets if ordered. Wine can be brought in. **Light suppers** if ordered.
1 Sitting-room. With open fire, central heating, TV.
Large garden.
Closed in December and January.

A gracious, sandstone-built Georgian hunting-lodge, Lawhill House is set among rolling farmland bounded on the north by a Roman road on which signal stations are still visible, and on the south by the River Earn, which here carves its way through the 'Valley of the Geese', so called because of the vast flocks of greylags which pass across the sky in season. The view from this side of the house, over the valley to the Ochil Hills beyond, is as lovely as any in this book, and the house is worthy of its setting.

In one vast sitting-room, sometimes available to guests, the wood-block floor and primrose walls set off to perfection the old leather furniture and a collection of commemorative mugs on the mantel over the open fire. And the dining-room is magnificent, with coffee-and-white walls and a huge mahogany dining-table surrounded by Georgian chairs and sideboard. Appropriately, dinner is served by candlelight.

Upstairs, bedrooms vary in size but not in quality; oatmeal carpets cover the floors and the colour schemes are delightful – yellow in the spacious family room, pink stripes in another. Elegant antiques predominate; a shower-room has been built into a roomy cupboard, and the bathroom is particularly good.

Diana Buchanan's cooking lays special emphasis on fresh, lightly cooked vegetables and home produce such as joints of her farmer son's lamb accompanied by potatoes with garlic and cream, or pasta. Fish and salads are also popular. Oatcakes and home-baked bread appear at breakfast, as (if ordered) might kippers and kedgeree.

There has been a settlement at Trinity Gask (not marked on all road maps) for over 900 years, and the origins of its tiny church are thought to date back to the time of St Columba (6th century). The area has historic connections with William Wallace (Gascon House) and Bonnie Prince Charlie (Tullibardine Castle).

LENDRUM FARM
Birkenhills, Aberdeenshire, AB53 8HA (Grampian)
Tel: 01888 544285
South-east of Turriff. Nearest main road: A947 from Turriff to Aberdeen.

2 Bedrooms. £15 (less for 5 nights). One has own bath/shower/toilet. Views of garden, country. No smoking. Washing machine on request.
Dinner (if ordered). £10 for 3 courses and coffee at 6–7.30pm. Non-residents not admitted. Vegetarian or special diets if ordered. Wine can be brought in.
Light suppers if ordered.
1 Sitting-room. With central heating, TV, record-player.
Small garden.

When Liberal chancellor David Lloyd George brought in the National Insurance Act in 1911, he began a process which catapulted Lendrum to national notoriety and a local fame which persists to this day. The farmer here, one Robert Patterson, felt that he looked after his workers well enough not to have to pay the government to look after them too, so he didn't. In 1913 the bailiffs came to Lendrum and seized a cow, intending to auction it in Turriff and set the proceeds against Patterson's unpaid National Insurance contributions. All the local farmers gave their men the day off in support of Patterson, and the resulting riots stopped the auction and made the national papers. Next the cow was taken to Aberdeen, where it wasn't sold either, and eventually it was returned to Lendrum. Today a plaque by the farm entrance commemorates the 'Turra Coo' (Turriff cow), and its place in local history is assured.

The Roebucks came here five years ago from Derbyshire, where Simon ran a firm selling animal health products. Now they work a mixed farm producing cattle, sheep and arable crops, and Christina offers bed-and-breakfast in the 19th-century farmhouse, where board doors and a narrow, twisting staircase enhance the traditional atmosphere. In the sitting-room are fine antiques and all-embracing red velvet sofa and armchairs; the bedrooms have delightful views over farmland and the neighbouring Fyvie estate.

Breakfast includes porridge, oatcakes, and a local speciality, Aberdeen butteries ('a cross between a croissant and flaky pastry' – delicious). By arrangement, Christina serves such dinners as home-made vegetable soup, roast lamb and pineapple meringue pudding.

This is an ideal place to get away from it all – the Roebucks' daughter had passed her driving test before she had to negotiate a single roundabout or set of traffic lights – but there is much to see too. Fyvie, with splendid church and castle (NTS), is close, and there are many other castles, distilleries, National Trust properties and beautiful coastline within easy reach.

LERAGS HOUSE
Lerags, by Oban, Argyll, PA34 4SE (Strathclyde)
Tel: 01631 63381
South of Oban. Nearest main road: A816 from Oban to Lochgilphead.

8 Bedrooms. £18–£20. Prices go up in May. Bargain breaks. All have own bath/shower/toilet. Tea/coffee facilities. Views of garden, country, loch. Washing machine on request.
Dinner. £9 for 3 courses and coffee at 7pm. Non-residents not admitted. Vegetarian or special diets if ordered. Wine can be brought in. No smoking.
Light suppers if ordered.
1 Sitting-room. With open fire, central heating, TV, piano.
Large garden.

Lerags means layers of land, and from the other side of Loch Feochan it is possible to distinguish the strata which gave the glen its name. The house could be said to be layered too, since the original building dates from 1325 (there are deeds to prove it) and the main structure was built by Alexander Campbell, a nephew of the Earl of Argyll, in the 17th century. The Georgian front was added in 1749; a two-storey conservatory fell down around 1900.

Doug and Freda Macleod came here in the late 1980s, though Doug, an educational psychologist, still works in Birmingham in the winter. Freda, a former personnel officer with a local health authority, loves cooking for her guests, and produces such homely meals as pâté or home-made soup followed by beef in red wine or chicken in a prawn-and-tarragon sauce, and home-made lemon meringue pie or cranachan (fruit, cream and toasted oatmeal).

As well as six upstairs bedrooms, varying in size but all pleasantly furnished, with cream paintwork and lovely garden views, there are two suites on the ground floor, with cosy sitting-rooms and pink bathrooms. Hall and family sitting-room are well stocked with books, and wooden shutters and an open fire make the dining-room equally welcoming.

There are otters in the glen: Gavin Maxwell's *Ring of Bright Water* was filmed here. In the space of ten minutes, Doug has seen peregrine falcons, buzzards, red kite and a white-tailed eagle; and wild cats live in the woods.

Oban (ferries to the islands) is close, and within easy reach is Inveraray Castle, where Lerags House is mentioned in a display of the branches of clan Campbell. Also at Inveraray is the award-winning Jail, where guides dressed as warders or prisoners demonstrate day-to-day life in the 19th-century prison; and the Scottish Salmon and Seafood Centre (exhibition, restaurant and shop) at Kilninver is worth a visit too.

THE LINNS   **C D M P T S X**
Kirk Lane, Blair Drummond, by Stirling, FK9 4AN (Central)
Tel: 01786 841679
South-west of Dunblane. Nearest main road: A84 from Stirling to Lochearnhead (and M9, junction 10).

3 Bedrooms. £16–£18 (less for 2 nights or continental breakfast; further reduction for 7 nights). One has own shower/toilet. Tea/coffee facilities. TV. Views of garden, country. Washing machine on request.
Light suppers if ordered.
2 Sitting-rooms. With open fire, central heating, TV. No smoking.
Garden.

There is a flat stretch of land – Blairdrummond Moss – just outside Stirling, which is bounded on the north by the River Teith and to the south by the Forth. In this fertile spot three 19th-century cottages have been converted and extended to form an L-shaped bungalow where Yorkshire-bred Pat and Bill Darby offer bed-and-breakfast, particularly to travellers breaking the long journey north.

In the old part of the house, the pine-clad ceilings in the spotless bedrooms contrast with the roof of the sitting-room, open to the rafters; guests may breakfast here if they wish, or join others in the modern wing, where two more bedrooms are neatly furnished and have attractive colour schemes. The bathroom here has a vast brown tub to stand in as you shower; every corner is immaculate, and, since there are never more than six people staying at any one time, a couple in the old wing is likely to have sole use of the sitting-room and good shower-room there.

The Darbys offer light suppers only, since most visitors prefer to dine at one of the numerous good eating-places nearby. There is a particularly good restaurant, with stunning views, at Kippen, six miles away.

Besides being conveniently close to a major south-north route from Carlisle and Glasgow to Inverness, The Linns is a good base from which to explore an area rich in interest and variety. Stirling is close, with the Victorian Wallace Monument commemorating the hero of the battle of Stirling Bridge (1297), where William Wallace defeated the English army (sent to relieve besieged Dundee) before going on to invade Cumberland and Northumberland.

To the west lies the Queen Elizabeth Forest Park, with visitor centre and forest trails; Loch Katrine and the Trossachs are only half an hour away.

LITTLE LODGE M
North Erradale, Wester Ross, IV21 2DS (Highland)
Tel: 01445 85237

North-west of Gairloch. Nearest main road: A832 from Braemore Junction to Garve.

3 Bedrooms. £35.50 **including dinner** (less for 3 nights; further reduction for 7 nights). Prices go up in April. All have own shower/toilet. Tea/coffee facilities. Views of garden, country, sea. No smoking. Washing machine on request.
Dinner. 3 courses (with choices) and coffee at 7pm. Non-residents not admitted. Vegetarian or special diets if ordered. Wine can be brought in. No smoking.
1 Sitting-room. With log stove, central heating, TV, record-player. No smoking.
Garden and croftland.
Closed from mid-December to end January.

It happens sometimes that a house, its situation, and the charm of its proprietors combine to create something quite outstanding: Little Lodge is by no means the only example of this happy concatenation in this book, but it is a splendid one. Di Johnson and Inge Ford moved here from Bristol in 1991, leaving behind their respective jobs as family therapist and infant-school Head, and have transformed the croft house into an idyllic setting for themselves and their guests. The sitting-room is a warm haven of stone and pine, with a log-burning stove, William Morris curtains, and chairs and a chaise longue upholstered in russet velvet to match the carpet and the single hessian wall. From the dining-room extension, one looks out to the Torridon Hills or over to Skye and the Cuillin, with Lewis and Harris beyond.

The immaculate bedrooms – one on the ground floor – are furnished in tones of russet and peach, with pine or white-painted fittings and cork-tiled shower-rooms. The views are dramatic.

Meals, too, are outstanding: breakfast offerings include apricot purée, figs, home-made muesli and locally smoked fish; dinner might start with parsnip, lemon and ginger soup or savoury avocado gratin; continue with locally caught salmon, or pork cooked with mushrooms, lemon and thyme; and finish with yogurt cream infused with cardamom seeds and served with strawberry purée.

All the loaves are home-made, vegetables home-grown whenever possible, and eggs from the croft's own hens – for Inge and Di are continuing the crofting tradition, keeping cashmere goats and Wensleydale and brown Shetland sheep, whose wool Inge spins on the old-fashioned wheel in the sitting-room.

The west coast boasts some of Scotland's finest scenery, as well as the best-known of its many excellent botanic gardens: Inverewe, magnificent at rhododendron time (May and June).

LOCHARTHUR HOUSE
Beeswing, Dumfries, DG2 8JG (Dumfries & Galloway)
Tel: 01387 760235
South-west of Dumfries. Off A711 from Dumfries to Dalbeattie.

2 Bedrooms. £15–£17 (less for 6 nights). Both have own bath/shower/toilet. Tea/coffee facilities. TV. Views of garden, country, loch. Washing machine on request.
Dinner. £6.50 for 3 courses and coffee at times to suit guests. Non-residents not admitted. Vegetarian or special diets if ordered. Wine can be brought in. No smoking. **Light suppers** if ordered.
1 Sitting-room. With central heating, TV, piano, record-player.
Large garden.

If **Paramount** (see elsewhere) is probably the only house in Scotland named for a ram, Beeswing seems likely to be the only village called after a racehorse. Between 1834 and 1842 the noble beast won 51 of 64 major races, inspiring locals to nickname a pub in Lochend 'the Beeswing'; the name stuck, widened its scope, and became the village of Beeswing.

Locharthur House was built by a Derbyshire engineer in 1840 as a summer home. Chris and Charles Schooling came here in 1980 when Charles was offered a job by the local water authority. Chris offers short courses in making jewellery and decorative panels of stained glass to hang against the light: you can see the effect in the pink-and-white dining-room, where Chris serves homely meals using fresh produce and vegetables from the garden whenever possible. A typical dinner might start with home-made soup or egg mayonnaise followed by a roast or a casserole, and end with a satisfying pudding like apple crumble or steamed syrup sponge.

The bedrooms are delightful, with lovely views of Loch Arthur and Lotus Hill, Laura Ashley or Sanderson fabrics and some fine old furniture (brass bedsteads in one). There is a large bathroom with very pretty iris tiles, where bright curtains and a low pine-clad ceiling create a cosy atmosphere despite its size.

This corner of Kirkcudbrightshire is a lovely and often underrated area. Five miles across country from Beeswing is New Abbey, where you can see the ruins of Sweetheart Abbey, a working corn mill, and a costume museum at Shambellie House. Dumfries has Robert Burns's house and mausoleum, and a Burns visitor centre, and there are miles of sandy beaches along the Solway coast. At Kirkbean is the cottage where John Paul Jones, 'father of the American navy', was born in 1747.

LOCHEND FARM
Carronbridge, Stirlingshire, FK6 5JJ (Central)
Tel: 01324 822778
North-west of Denny. Nearest main road: A872 from Stirling to Denny (and M9/M80, junction 9).

2 Bedrooms. £16.50–£17.50 (less for 8 nights). Tea/coffee facilities. Views of garden, country. No smoking. Washing machine on request.
Light suppers if ordered.
1 Sitting-room. With central heating, TV.
Small garden.
Closed from November to Easter (except by arrangement).

Harebells star the banks of the lane leading to this attractive 18th-century stone farmhouse, but even they can't lessen the impact of the spectacular sunken garden that greets visitors in the centre of the square farmyard. Finding that the air here was too pure to allow her roses to flourish (black spot was rarely seen in the industrial north-west of England before the passing of the Clean Air Act), Jean Morton has planted a well-chosen selection of plants and shrubs for year-round interest and colour in what used to be the farm midden; in former days barrowloads of manure were wheeled from the byres lining the yard and tipped into the three-foot pit.

Indoors, the colours are just as striking: the hall is regally purple and gold, and the bathroom, with its damson carpet and aquamarine suite, is a delight. Bedrooms are comfortable too, with lovely views over the Pentland Hills, and Jean's handiwork is visible in the tapestries on the walls and the home-made lampshades.

Breakfasts are plentiful; bread is sometimes home-baked, and porridge is always on the menu. Jean serves light suppers only, but for dinner directs visitors to **Topps Farm** (see elsewhere) or to the Cross Keys at Kippen, where the view is almost as rewarding as the food.

Lochend Farm, which overlooks Loch Coulter, is within easy reach of Edinburgh and Glasgow, yet less than an hour from Loch Lomond and the Trossachs. Across Kincardine Bridge, Culross Palace (NTS) reopened in 1994 after a two-year renovation and is fully on display for the first time since 1932.

Houses which accept the discount vouchers on page ii are marked with a V on the regional list, see pages xiii-xvi.

LOCHSIDE COTTAGE CDMS
Fasnacloich, Appin, Argyll, PA38 4BJ (Strathclyde)
Tel: 01631 73216 (changing to 01631 730216)
North-east of Oban. Nearest main road: A828 from Ballachulish to Connel.

3 Bedrooms. £18–£20. All have own bath/shower/toilet. Tea/coffee facilities. TV. Views of garden, country, loch. No smoking. Washing machine on request.
Dinner. £15 for 4 courses (with choices) and coffee at 7.30pm. Non-residents not admitted. Vegetarian or special diets if ordered. Wine can be brought in. No smoking. **Light suppers** if ordered.
1 Sitting-room. With open fire, central heating, piano, record-player. No smoking.
Large garden.

From the main coast road between Oban and Fort William, a small turning up Glen Creran takes you very quickly into the kind of wild and remote-seeming countryside which is never far away in the west of Scotland. Then, before the road peters out altogether, the ground dips away to where Lochside Cottage nestles a few yards from the shore of Loch Baile Mhic Chailen, traditionally a border between Campbell and Stewart land.

The situation is spectacular; across the loch, Beinn Sgulaird rises to over 3000 feet; and there is a spot beyond the trees from which you can see the hills of Glencoe, ten miles away. At the back of the house the hillside is covered with bluebell woods, and in May the glen is vibrant with rhododendrons.

Earle and Stella Broadbent moved up here in the late 1980s, when they gave up the prep school they used to run in Hampshire. Earle – a Scot – now works as a civil engineer in Oban, while Stella concentrates her considerable talents on looking after their guests: her cooking is outstanding, and dinner is always an event. It might start with a choice of smokies, bacon and croûton salad, or an unusual soup like cucumber or watercress, and finish with Scottish cheeses (served with home-made oatcakes) after a pudding like chocolate mousse or fruit pavlova. For the main course, local produce like salmon or venison is used as much as possible; and for those who prefer it grilled trout is always available.

One of the two ground-floor bedrooms overlooks the loch, and both have (like the rest of the house) lots of pictures. The upstairs bedroom, though, is particularly attractive: long and low, it has a sitting-area at one end and a pine-panelled bathroom. There is a Blüthner grand piano in the upstairs sitting-room, and a particularly comfortable sofa and chairs upholstered in Liberty fabric from which to enjoy those glorious views.

LOW COYLTON HOUSE C D PT
Manse Road, Coylton, Ayrshire, KA6 6LE (Strathclyde)
Tel: 01292 570615
East of Ayr. Nearest main road: A70 from Ayr to Edinburgh.

3 Bedrooms. £34.50 **including dinner** (less for 8 nights). All have own bath/shower/toilet. Tea/coffee facilities. TV. Views of garden, country, river. Washing machine on request.
Dinner. 3 courses and coffee at 6.30–7.30pm. Non-residents not admitted. Vegetarian or special diets if ordered. Wine can be brought in. **Light suppers** if ordered.
1 Sitting-room. With open fire, central heating, TV.
Large garden.

The last minister left this former Church of Scotland manse in 1975; not so long before that, miners who couldn't afford to hire the church were still being married in what is now the dining-room of this gracious 19th-century house.

George and Anne Hay came here in the 1980s, and have created an atmosphere of unobtrusive elegance. Ceilings are high, cornices elaborate; colour schemes are imaginative and pleasing, ranging from palest pink and blue in the sitting-room to a cheerful red-and-green bathroom off a pretty bedroom with delicately patterned pink wallpaper, flowery covers on the wooden bed, and lovely views. The blue bedroom has pine beds and a glorious bathroom with green-and-pink Chinese-style wallpaper and a pine-clad ceiling. There is a very attractive peach-and-blue room, with bleached wooden units and a good shower-room with gaily painted mirror-frames.

On one wall of the dining-room hangs Anne's collection of blue Royal Copenhagen 'Hans Christian Andersen' Christmas plates – one for each year since 1970. A portrait of her great-grandfather looks on as guests enjoy such dinners as carrot-and-coriander soup or a pear with Stilton; salmon béarnaise or chicken en croûte; and whisky-and-honey mousse or lemon soufflé.

Anne, who came to Britain from Denmark in the 1960s, is a delightful host, warm and friendly, with (if pressed) a fund of stories about her days as a publicist for Opera West. Amazingly, she still manages to fit a great deal of charity work around her attention to her guests.

Ayr, with its Burns connections and Tam o' Shanter Museum, is a few minutes away; Ardrossan (ferry to Arran) within 25 miles. Glasgow (the Burrell Collection) can be reached in ¾ hour, Culzean Castle in perhaps half that time. But there are more rural attractions too: miles of sandy beaches along the Firth of Clyde, and southwards the Galloway Forest Park and lovely Glen Trool.

MACKEANSTON HOUSE   C D X
Doune, Perthshire, FK16 6AX (Central)   Tel: 01786 850213
West of Dunblane. Nearest main road: A84 from Stirling to Lochearnhead.

2 Bedrooms. £19–£20. Prices go up in May. Both have own bath/shower/toilet. Tea/coffee facilities. TV. Views of garden, country. No smoking. Washing machine on request.
Dinner (by arrangement). £12 for 3 courses and coffee from 7pm. Non-residents not admitted. Vegetarian or special diets if ordered. Wine can be brought in. **Light suppers** if ordered.
1 Sitting-room. With open fire, central heating, TV.
Large garden.

Readers of the *England and Wales* edition of this book will feel at home here: Fiona and Colin Graham have used the book for years, and there are copies on display in the guest bedrooms.

There has been a house on this site since the early 17th century; the present handsome farmhouse was bought by Colin's father, General Freddie Graham, in 1947 and has been renovated to a very high standard. On the first floor, the yellow room (with cane bedhead, pretty loveknot fabrics and a primrose bathroom) feels sunny whatever the weather; the master bedroom has a canopy over the bed and an outstanding bathroom. You can see the Gargunnock Hills and Stirling Castle, ten miles away, from the windows.

Down the graceful wooden staircase, the polished oak table in the kitchen/dining-room glows against deep peach walls; this is where guests usually relax on winter evenings, though the Grahams sometimes offer the use of their own drawing-room, beautifully furnished with antiques and fine paintings.

In the kitchen, Fiona uses as many home-grown vegetables and fruit as possible, and makes all her own jams, jellies and marmalade. A typical dinner might be carrot-and-lentil soup (served with home-baked malted wholemeal bread), pork-and-prune casserole with Basmati rice, and home-made strawberry ice cream with fresh strawberries.

Doune, less than eight miles from the M9 motorway and thus easily accessible from Glasgow, Edinburgh and all points south, is also close to some of the most beautiful scenery in Scotland: Loch Katrine and the Trossachs are close, and wild 'Rob Roy country'.

Far from the romantic hero of fiction, Rob Roy (Red Robert) MacGregor was something of an 18th-century Godfather, extorting payment from Lowland farmers whose stock he 'protected' from the depredations of lawless Highlanders. At the battle of Sheriffmuir in 1715 he took no part in the fighting, apparently only interested in the booty; and in 1716 he became an outlaw following financial losses.

MAGDALENE HOUSE   PT
Lochmaben, Dumfriesshire, DG11 1PD (Dumfries & Galloway)
Tel: 01387 810439
West of Lockerbie. On A709 from Lockerbie to Dumfries.

rear view

4 Bedrooms. £18–£21 (less for 2 nights). Bargain breaks. Three have own bath/shower/toilet. Tea/coffee facilities. TV. Views of garden, town. No smoking. Washing machine on request.
Dinner. £15 for 5 courses and coffee at 7.30pm. Non-residents not admitted. Vegetarian or special diets if ordered. Wine can be brought in. No smoking.
2 Sitting-rooms. With open fire, central heating, TV, piano. No smoking (in one).
Garden.

The elegant façade set slightly back from the road in the historic little town of Lochmaben is promising, but even so gives little hint of the different and very special nature of a stay in this 18th-century house (built over a 14th-century cellar). For in this former Church of Scotland manse, now the home of chieftain McKerrell of Hillhouse and the Lady Hillhouse, guests are invited to choose between a bed-and-breakfast arrangement or 'the Georgian house party', when groups of two to six people are entertained in almost forgotten luxury, met from train or aeroplane and taken for daily tours of the lovely border countryside in a large and comfortable Renault, and brought home in time to bath and change before dinner.

Charles and May dine with their guests under the benign gaze of Charles's ancestors whose portraits line the walls, polished silver gleaming on white linen, candlelight refracted by the glass. Emphasis is on the best of local produce, and a typical dinner might be smoked salmon, cream of broccoli soup, a taste of haggis, roast lamb or baked salmon served with fresh vegetables or salad, and raspberries with Drambuie cream. Scottish cheeses are offered to anyone with space left for them.

Two bedrooms have four-posters, one has a cheerful red bathroom; all are bright with wood and cane, Sanderson paper or antique cream-and-gilt furniture. A Broadwood grand piano graces the sitting-room, with French windows opening onto the lovely walled garden; outside the pink-walled library hangs a copy of Robert Burns's poem to 'The Blue-eyed Lassie', which was written in this house for the daughter of the poet's friend Andrew Jaffrey, minister here at the time.

Mary Queen of Scots visited Lochmaben Castle and called it 'a lovely place, the very home of beauty'. And it was to his seat in Lochmaben that an earlier monarch, Robert Bruce, came in 1306 to tell his wife that she was queen of Scotland.

MAINS OF SOILZARIE
Bridge of Cally, Perthshire, PH10 7LS (Tayside)
Tel: 01250 881222
North of Blairgowrie. Nearest main road: A93 from Blairgowrie to Aberdeen.

2 Bedrooms. £20 (less for 5 nights). Both have own bath/shower/toilet. Tea/coffee facilities. TV. Views of garden, country. No smoking. Washing machine on request.
Dinner (by arrangement). £12 for 3 courses and coffee from 7.30pm. Non-residents not admitted. Vegetarian or special diets if ordered. Wine can be brought in. No smoking. **Light suppers** if ordered.
2 Sitting-rooms. With open fire, central heating, TV. No smoking.
Large garden.
Closed from October to March.

Sara Jane Gilbey is quick to help hesitant English visitors with the pronunciation of the name of her beautiful house: it's Solyarry, believed to derive from an old Celtic word *solleir*, meaning bright, and indeed this is one of the driest areas of Scotland, renowned for its soft fruit which spills from farm shops, roadside stalls and pick-your-own fields throughout the summer. Originally an 18th-century bothy, the Mains is now one of the most elegant houses in this book, with fine paintings complementing the antique furniture, and in the gracious sitting-room a splendid gilt-framed mirror reflecting lots of comfortable chairs in which to absorb the beauty of the surroundings.

Upstairs are more pictures, even in the bathrooms – from one of which, however, the view of Mount Blair is so breathtaking that it is difficult to drag one's eyes from the window. One room is pink, another yellow; the double room with old cane bedhead gets the morning sun.

Breakfast is served in the conservatory, with its spectacular view across the valley, and Sara Jane's collection of colourful and interesting plates; the menu offers porridge, smoked haddock, kippers and a variety of teas, while bread, jam, marmalade and scones are home-made. Dinner, which is served by arrangement only, might comprise pâté or soup, local salmon either smoked or fresh, and fruit pavlova or peaches in wine. Sara Jane can recommend a variety of pubs and restaurants on nights when dinner is not available, several within ten minutes' drive.

Set in the midst of beautiful countryside, Mains of Soilzarie is nevertheless within easy reach of such attractions as Glamis Castle, childhood home of the Queen Mother, Scone Palace, where Scottish kings were crowned, and Blair Castle, where the Duke of Atholl maintains the only remaining private army in Britain: 24 men and a piper.

MARCH HOUSE
Feshiebridge, Kincraig, Inverness-shire, PH21 1NG (Highland)
Tel: 01540 651388
North-east of Kingussie. Nearest main road: A9 from Inverness to Perth.

6 Bedrooms. £16–£18 (less for 3 nights). Prices go up in May. Bargain breaks. All have own bath/shower/toilet. Tea/coffee facilities. Views of garden, country. No smoking. Washing machine on request.
Dinner. £12 for 3 courses and coffee at 7pm. Vegetarian or special diets if ordered. Wine can be brought in. **Light suppers** if ordered.
1 Sitting-room. With open fire, central heating, piano, record-player.
Garden.
Closed from November to 27 December.

Making people welcome is in Caroline Hayes's blood: you feel it even before you realise that not only does her sister run **Old Pines** (see elsewhere), but their mother offers bed-and-breakfast in an oast-house in Sussex. Caroline is a delightful hostess, sometimes teaching guests to spin on the carved wooden wheel in the sitting-room. Her knots of dried grasses or moss adorn bedroom doors, and there are always flowers around the house – Caroline's arrangements of home-dried ones, when fresh blooms aren't available.

Each bedroom has a theme, echoed in pictures, tiles and fabrics: there is the rose room, the thistle room, the goose room, and – endearingly – the poppy-and-puffin room. All have breathtaking views of the Cairngorms and Glen Feshie; most visitors come here to walk, climb or (in winter) ski, and maps of the area are always available for consultation. Birdwatching is popular too, and there is a gliding club just down the track.

For dinner, it is Ernie who does most of the cooking, leaving only the puddings to Caroline. She also makes wholemeal soda rolls to accompany his home-made soups and pâtés; for main courses he makes use of fresh local produce including trout, venison and lamb. Pudding might be raspberry-and-apple pie with oatmeal pastry, crème brûlée, or whisky cream.

The house – built as a guest-house in 1980 – lies right at the foot of the Cairngorm mountains, on the edge of the National Nature Reserve. Close by is Loch an Eilein, where you can still see the ruins of the 14th-century island castle of the infamous 'Wolf of Badenoch', brother of Robert III; more recent history is commemorated at Ruthven Barracks near Kingussie, where the defeated Jacobites assembled after the disaster of Culloden in 1746.

MILLER'S FIELD M PT S
Dalginross, Comrie, Perthshire, PH6 2HE (Tayside)
Tel: 01764 670073
West of Crieff. Nearest main road: A85 from Oban to Dundee.

rear view

2 Bedrooms. £15–£16 (less for 4 nights). Tea/coffee facilities. Views of garden, country. No smoking. Washing machine on request.
Light suppers for very late arrivals only.
2 Sitting-rooms. With open fire, central heating, TV. No smoking.
Small garden.

Not a converted mill but an architect-designed 1980s bungalow built in Mr Miller's field, Miller's Field is set well back from the road on the outskirts of Comrie, a little town not far from either Perth or Stirling but within easy reach of the glorious scenery of the Grampian highlands too.

Helen and Gordon Rae came here from Edinburgh in 1990 and fell in love with the place – an enthusiasm they pass on to their guests, many of whom return time and again. Breakfast is taken in the glass-roofed conservatory, which looks onto the pretty garden (and populous bird-table close to the windows); the side walls are whitewashed brick, the inner one clad in blue-painted pine. Two vast, embracing armchairs take up much of the quarry-tiled floor, and it is with reluctance that guests sometimes have to retreat from the sun into the Raes' comfortable sitting-room, with its William Morris sofa and chairs, Victorian cast-iron fireplace (from a Glasgow tenement), and walls covered with interesting prints beautifully framed and displayed.

The bedrooms are particularly attractive, with Laura Ashley paper, pine beds and lovely views, while the blue-and-white bathroom is a delight, its brass taps gleaming in the sunlight. (For those who prefer a shower, the Raes offer the use of their own, at the other end of the house.)

Helen does not provide evening meals, but there are two hotels in the town – the Royal and the Comrie – which serve good food; and excellent bar suppers are available at Achray House, St Fillan, on nearby Loch Earn.

Lochearnhead and the picture-postcard town of Killin, with the famous Falls of Dochart, are close; climbers make for Ben Lawers (with visitor centre and nature trail), whisky drinkers for Glenturret Distillery near Crieff, Scotland's oldest – and once the home of the legendary Towser, mouse-catcher extraordinary.

Readers' comments: Delightful couple, beautiful bungalow in a lovely area; immaculate; the décor is delightful.

MILTON FARM

C(10) PT S X

Leuchars, St Andrews, Fife, KY16 0AB   Tel: 01334 839281
North-west of St Andrews. Nearest main road: A919 from A91 to Carrick.

2 **Bedrooms.** £18–£20 (less for 3 nights). Both have own bath/shower/toilet. Views of garden, country, sea. No smoking. Washing machine on request.
Light suppers if ordered.
1 **Sitting-room.** With open fire, central heating, TV. No smoking.
Large garden.

Leuchars – the name means 'place of rushes' – is better known for its RAF base than as a holiday centre, so the attractions of the area in its own right, as well as its convenience for St Andrews in one direction and Dundee in the other, come as a pleasant surprise.

Milton Farm is set amid rolling arable land above the town, a gracious Georgian farmhouse filled with fine old furniture and family treasures. Guests take breakfast in the sitting-room, high-ceilinged and elegant, with pink walls and chairs to set off the pale green carpet and slate hearth, a display of china in a white-painted alcove, and richly moulded cornices.

Upstairs, the green bedroom has bright rosy fabrics and splendid 1930s satinwood wardrobe and chest of drawers; both rooms have good, firm beds, and each has sole use of either the blue-and-white shower-room or the pretty pink bathroom – the first visitors to book are given the choice.

Helen Black does not serve dinners, for there are several good eating-places nearby, not least in St Andrews – a city which deserves lengthy exploration. The cathedral ruins and the castle, the famous golf courses (and numerous golf shops, exhibitions, etc.) and just the hilly streets themselves can be wandered for hours – especially if one has already discovered the award-winning ice cream shop. A more unusual attraction is the underground Secret Bunker, once a nuclear shelter for British government ministers.

At Leuchars itself, don't neglect to visit 16th-century Earlshall Castle and gardens; Mary Queen of Scots slept here. The Scottish Deer Centre near Cupar is practical enough to offer the loan of umbrellas to those who want to explore the park as well as enjoy its many indoor facilities. And why not take the train from Leuchars to Dundee, across – in the words of the immortal William McGonagall – 'the beautiful new railway bridge of the Silvery Tay . . . the greatest railway bridge of the present day'?

MONTCOFFER HOUSE CDS
Banff, AB45 3LJ (Grampian)   Tel: 01261 812979
Nearest main road: A947 from Banff to Turriff.

3 Bedrooms. £16. All have own bath/shower/toilet. Tea/coffee facilities. TV (in one). Views of garden, country, river. No smoking. Washing machine on request.
Dinner. £7.50 for 3 courses (with some choices) and coffee at 6.30–8pm. Non-residents not admitted. Vegetarian or special diets if ordered. Wine can be brought in. No smoking. **Light suppers** if ordered.
3 Sitting-rooms. With open fire, central heating, TV, record-player. No smoking in two.
Large garden.
Closed in November.

Of all the memorable features of Montcoffer House, it is a clock which stands out: look carefully at the one on the sitting-room wall next to the door into the library. . . it might surprise you.

And when you contemplate the magnificent mirror on the far wall of the library itself, you might consider that, were it not for the fact that the room was used to stack bales of straw in the 1960s and early '70s, the mirror might not have survived. Those were the house's darkest days; in 1976 the work of restoration began, and 14 years later Alec and Dorothy Clark bought a house of dreams.

Originally built in 1680, it had been extended in 1825 (when it was part of the Fyvie estate), but allowed to deteriorate until it was sold by the estate in 1960. The Clarks have researched its history and put together a fascinating leaflet through which guests can browse before or after one of Dorothy's homely dinners, which might comprise a starter of haggis, neeps (turnips) and tatties (potatoes), or Yorkshire pudding and gravy; a roast, or local fish; and a pudding like crumble, gâteau or fresh fruit salad.

Upstairs, views are spectacular, over the garden to the vale of Deveron. In one bedroom, though, the focus of interest is closer: an unusually fine cut-leaved beech practically taps the window and would draw the eye even without its complement of colourful tits and finches; while outside the en suite bathroom are the octagonal roofs of the old game and fish larders.

All the bedrooms are large and comfortable; the bathrooms are stunning, with suites in green, pink and puce. In the attic, Dorothy – who used to run a nursery school – has created a safe and well-equipped playroom.

A local beauty-spot is the Bridge of Alvah, and Montcoffer House lies directly on the path to it. Duff House at Banff and the museum at Macduff are also worth a visit.

NETHER BORELAND FARM
Boreland, Dumfriesshire, DG11 2LL (Dumfries & Galloway)
Tel: 01576 610248
North of Lockerbie. Nearest main road: A74 from Abington to M6 and Carlisle.

3 Bedrooms. From £18 (less for 4 nights). All have own bath/shower/toilet. Tea/coffee facilities. TV. Views of country, river. No smoking. Washing machine on request.
Light suppers only.
1 Sitting-room. With central heating, TV.
Small garden.
Closed from December to February.

Always on the lookout for ways to keep her visitors happy, Marjorie Rae has hit on the idea of making her own local videos, which she edits herself. Now she rarely goes out without her camera, so she had it with her the day she captured on film her *pièce de résistance:* the Great Cygnet Rescue. While the camcorder whirred, her husband Bob and others attempted to catch the wandering fledgeling and restore it to its anxious parents. Charlie Chaplin couldn't have done it better.

The oldest part of the house, where the walls are 3½ feet thick, dates from the 16th century. Once a coaching inn, it was a popular pub or 'howff' between the wars: the landlady, Peggy Hayes, is still remembered for her tendency to 'send men home steaming'! No doubt to their wives' relief, the licensing authorities decided Boreland was too remote for police surveillance and the pub was closed. Now Nether Boreland is a 200-acre farm rearing beef and lamb.

The two front bedrooms, with views of the farm and the Dryfe Valley, are in the original part of the house. The room at the back looks over the sheep-shed – a sought-after prospect at lambing time. The sitting-room downstairs blends shades of fawn and peach into a restful whole; paintings of local scenes and tapestries by Marjorie's mother hang on the walls.

On the splendid old sideboard in the dining-room, Bob grins out from a photograph of the Scottish curling team which toured Canada in January 1993. They won – the first time Scotland had beaten the Canadians in Canada since 1946. Surrounding the photograph are china animal figures from Border Fine Arts in Langholm – some of the farm cat and dog, and several of Texel sheep (a breed reared at Nether Boreland).

For breakfast, served on Royal Doulton china, kedgeree is usually available; eggy bread and haggis too. Marjorie serves light suppers only; guests dine in Moffat or Lockerbie, or at the excellent pub in Eskdalemuir.

NETHER COUL
Auchterarder, Perthshire, PH3 1ET (Tayside)
Tel: 01764 663119
Nearest main road: A9 from Perth to Dunblane.

2 Bedrooms. £13–£14 (less for 3 nights). Both have own bath/shower/toilet. Views of garden, country, river. No smoking. Washing machine on request.
Dinner. £8 for 3 courses (with some choices) and coffee at times to suit guests. Non-residents not admitted. Vegetarian or special diets if ordered. Wine can be brought in. No smoking.
Light suppers if ordered.
2 Sitting-rooms. With open fire, central heating, TV, piano, record-player. No smoking.
Large garden.

Nether Coul has come full circle: it started life in 1860 as a roadhouse on the old drove road between Perth and Stirling; now Stuart and Susie Robertson (she is an 18th great-granddaughter of Robert Bruce) welcome bed-and-breakfast visitors once more – though without the cattle. When they bought the house in 1979 it had no electricity or running water; rumour has it that the old lady who lived here before them hadn't had a bath for 60 years. Now, however, the green-and-cream bedroom has its own huge cork-tiled bathroom (with oval bath) downstairs; the pink family room, sole use of a well-equipped shower-room.

Downstairs, guests can relax in deep pink velvet sofas in the sitting-room, or bask in the sunroom at the front of the house.

Dinner might comprise grapefruit Wellington (baked with oranges, cherries, raw cane sugar and whisky), home-produced roast lamb with three vegetables, and fresh fruit salad with home-made ice cream and double cream. Afterwards, if you like, you can take to the croquet lawn in the extensive grounds and work off your aggressive instincts along with your meal.

There is always activity at Nether Coul; in the wood-floored hall hang medals and rosettes won by Susie and the children for shooting, skiing, swimming and riding.

The area was well known for its cloth industry, the dyeworks for which were situated within the grounds of Nether Coul. Auchterarder itself has a heritage centre which gives local history from mediaeval times. Further afield you can visit Scone Palace and the Caithness Glass works at Perth; Dunblane Cathedral; and Sheriffmuir, site of the last battle of 'the '15'. The fighting was inconclusive, but the next day the Earl of Mar's army was nowhere to be seen, and the Old Pretender's failure to claim the throne from George I was sealed.

NETHERTON FARM   C
Abington, Lanarkshire, ML12 6RU (Strathclyde)
Tel: 018642 321
South-west of Biggar. Nearest main road: A74 from Abington to M6 and Carlisle (and M74, junction 13).

3 Bedrooms. £13–£15 (less for 4 nights). One has own bath/shower/toilet. Tea/coffee facilities. Views of garden, country, river. No smoking. Washing machine on request.
Dinner. £6 for 3 courses (with some choices) and coffee at times to suit guests. Non-residents not admitted. Vegetarian or special diets if ordered. Wine can be brought in. No smoking.
Light suppers if ordered.
2 Sitting-rooms. With open fire, central heating, TV (in one), piano, record-player. Bar.
Garden.

Once owned by Sir Alec Douglas-Home, Netherton has been farmed by Hyslops for nearly 40 years. John and Lillias (whose lovely name also belonged to her mother and grandmother; her own eldest daughter is Lorna Lillias) took over when his father moved to **Glentewing Farm** (see elsewhere) in 1993. (Incidentally, Lillias must keep her wits about her: not only are her husband and son both called John – her father-in-law and *his* father too – but her brother and brother-in-law as well!)

The house was built as a shooting-lodge for Edward VII; propped up against the wall outside are stones on which 'Morning butt' and 'Afternoon butt' can still be deciphered, though the king himself never actually stayed here.

From the hall, an unusually wide and shallow staircase leads up to a spacious landing lit by a chandelier. Two of the bedrooms are huge, one, grey and pink, the other pink and pale green; both have windows on two sides to take advantage of the views. The farmhouse is on a slight rise between the M74 and a quiet B road; because of the prevailing wind direction, the motorway can hardly be heard at all up here.

Lillias uses as much local produce as possible in her cooking; beef and lamb from the farm, fresh vegetables from Lanark market. Soups and puddings are home-made. Her Scottish breakfast includes fried clootie dumpling (fruit pudding), potato scones or pancakes.

The area deserves more than a passing glance en route to Edinburgh and the north. Netherton sits at the bottom of the lovely Clyde Valley (fishing permits can be obtained); further north is Biggar, where you can visit the Greenhill Covenanter's House, and at Broughton is a gallery exhibiting works by leading British artists and craftsmen (glass, ceramics, turned and carved wood, traditional toys and jewellery for sale).

OLD MANSE   C D P T S
Fodderty, Ross-shire, IV14 9AB (Highland)   Tel: 01997 421209
West of Dingwall. On A834 from Dingwall to Strathpeffer.

2 Bedrooms. £13.50–£14.50 (less for 4 nights). Views of garden, country. No smoking. Washing machine on request.
Dinner. £7.50 for 3 courses and coffee at 8pm. Non-residents not admitted. Vegetarian or special diets if ordered. Wine can be brought in. No smoking.
Light suppers if ordered.
1 Sitting-room. With open fire, central heating, TV, record-player. No smoking.
Large garden.
Closed from November to March.

It is to be hoped that one at least of the Brahan Seer's prophecies does not come true, for if it does the Old Manse at Fodderty – and much else – will cease to exist. The Seer, a 17th-century farm labourer gifted with second sight – or so his disciples believe – is said to have foretold that ships would one day tie up again at the 'Eagle Stone': a local landmark which might indeed once have served as a mooring post when the Cromarty Firth extended beyond its present-day boundary over the low-lying land between.

The manse was built in 1794 for the minister of the nearby church (now a hotel). The graceful, pink sitting-room is beautifully proportioned and furnished; like the dining-room, it has a view of the Cat's Back, a ridge of land which proves irresistible to walkers. Upstairs, the blue room looks over the garden to the Strathpeffer golf links; from another, with brass bed and pink covers and walls, one can see the gate into a walled 'secret garden'. Both rooms have their original fireplaces, and attractive white-painted towel-rails and chairs.

By arrangement, Pauline Murray serves such dinners as home-made soup, salmon with oatmeal potatoes, and home-made lemon meringue pie. (Robert is in the salmon business, so the farmed fish, fresh or smoked, is often on the menu.) Breakfast includes such options as porridge, potato scones, black pudding, cheese, yogurt and fresh fruit. On evenings when no dinner is served, a supper of soup and toasted sandwiches is available in the sitting-room.

Strathpeffer is a Victorian spa village which offers, among other attractions, a museum of toys, dolls and Victoriana in the old station. Nearby is a monument to Neil Gunn, the Scottish novelist beloved for his descriptions of ordinary Highland life, who died in 1973.

OLD PIER HOUSE
Fort Augustus, Inverness-shire, PH32 4BX (Highland)
Tel: 01320 366418
Nearest main road: A82 from Inverness to Fort William.

Views of garden, country, loch. No smoking. Washing machine on request.
Dinner. £11–£12.50 for 3 courses and coffee at 7–8pm. Non-residents not admitted. Vegetarian or special diets if ordered. Wine can be ordered or brought in. No smoking. **Light suppers** if ordered.
1 Sitting-room. With open fire, central heating, TV, piano. No smoking.
Large garden.
Closed from November to March.

3 Bedrooms. £15–£25 (less for 8 nights). Prices go up in July and August. All have own bath/shower/toilet. Tea/coffee facilities.

When the piermaster's house was built here in 1880, the only way to get from this southern tip of Loch Ness to Inverness was by water: a single-track railway terminated at the pier and passengers went on by boat. In the other direction, the Caledonian Canal, opened in 1822, transported traffic down to Fort William and thence to Loch Linnhe and the open sea.

Now, of course, there are roads up and down either side of Loch Ness, the railway has gone, and when the MacKenzies came to Fort Augustus in the early 1970s the house had been derelict for years. In the hands of this talented family of linguists and musicians, it has been renovated to an impeccable standard, with stripped floorboards, white-painted walls, pine furniture and cotton bedlinen.

At mealtimes, the emphasis is on fresh local produce: eggs are free-range and beef is home-produced. All soups are vegetarian – tomato with grated orange and basil is delicious – and a favourite pudding is summer fruit pie, made with apples, redcurrants, bilberries, blackberries and raspberries. For the main course, Jenny might offer poached cod with shrimp sauce, salmon, trout, crofter's pie (meat and vegetables) or venison pie (with red wine and mushrooms). Breakfast might include prunes and apricots, yogurt, oatcakes and porridge.

It is hard to think of an activity which is not catered for at Old Pier House. There is a riding centre, and visitors are sometimes taken on evening boat trips to see the wildlife (otters, roe deer) on the opposite side of the loch. There is rowing to be had, and canoeing, and windsurfing; and mountain bikes to borrow. In addition, Jenny takes guests to see the Highland cattle (including a very rare white cow) in the MacKenzies' woods; she will also show you the best of the wildflowers in May and June, and edible mushrooms in the autumn.

Finally, no visit to Old Pier House is complete without an introduction to Dougal, the Shetland pony, who will unpack your car for a Polo mint!

OLD PINES   C D M P T S X
Spean Bridge, Inverness-shire, PH34 4EG (Highland)
Tel: 01397 712324
North-east of Fort William. Nearest main road: A82 from Fort William to Inverness.

8 Bedrooms. £20–£25 (less for 4 nights). All have own bath/shower/toilet. Tea/coffee facilities. Views of garden, country. No smoking. Washing machine on request.
Dinner. £17.50 for 4 courses (with alternatives) and coffee at 8pm. Vegetarian or special diets if ordered. Wine can be brought in. No smoking.
Light suppers if ordered.
2 Sitting-rooms. With open fire, central heating, TV, piano, record-player. No smoking.
Large garden.

If you stand at the front door of Old Pines on a clear day, you will see the skyline pierced by the unmistakable profile of Ben Nevis. There is an even more stunning view from the Commando Memorial a few hundred yards away, where an etched chart names the peaks and landmarks visible through 360 degrees. The memorial is itself a notable landmark: an impressive sculpture dedicated to the Commando units of the Second World War, and bearing the words 'This country was their training ground'.

Indoors, much use of wood and stone, white paint, pretty fabrics and fresh flowers has contributed to the prevailing atmosphere of lightness and comfort. The single-storey, Scandinavian-style guest-house was built at the end of the 1970s, and stands in 30 acres of wooded grounds – the old pines of its name are mature trees, not building materials!

Wood-burning stoves, family photographs and shelves of well-read books lend a homely air to the sitting-room; Sukie Scott has extended the dining-room into the conservatory, and it is here that guests enjoy the kind of cooking that won the regional award (and third prize over all) in the 1993 Taste of Scotland Lamb Challenge.

Dinner might start with a hot creamy soufflé of smoked haddock with a lemon-and-dill sauce, or a salad of pink grapefruit and Scottish cheese with a raspberry vinegar dressing. The main course might be venison with pineapple juice, thyme and juniper berries, or trout from Loch Lochy (caught that afternoon) stuffed with orange and leeks, served with fresh vegetables including potatoes baked with cream, garlic and nutmeg. For pudding you could be offered mixed berry brûlée, or raspberry trifle; and finally a selection of Scottish hand-made cheeses served with oatcakes. Most months, duck eggs are available for breakfast, along with porridge, prunes, yogurt, Cumberland or venison sausage, potato scones and kippers. A particularly popular choice is scrambled eggs with smoked trout.

OLD SMIDDY C D M P T S X
Laide, Wester Ross, IV22 2NB (Highland) Tel: 01445 731425
North-east of Gairloch. Nearest main road: A832 from A835 to Gairloch.

2 Bedrooms. £17.50–£19 (less for 6 nights). Both have own bath/shower/toilet. Tea/coffee facilities. Views of garden, country. No smoking. Washing machine on request.
Dinner. £13.50 for 3 courses (with choices) and coffee at 7–8pm. Vegetarian or special diets if ordered. Wine can be brought in. No smoking. **Light suppers** if ordered.
1 Sitting-room. With wood-burning stove, central heating, TV. No smoking. **Small garden.**

As befits a former smithy, the Old Smiddy sits directly on the main coastal route between Braemore Junction and Poolewe (Inverewe Gardens are near), but the road is rarely busy. Both bedrooms are delightful, but anyone worried about possible traffic noise might be happier in the blue-and-yellow family room built in the roof and reached by a twisting staircase with shower-room at its foot. On the ground floor, the blue-and-peach room has a blue-carpeted bathroom.

Elsewhere, the house is crammed with family treasures and fascinating pieces Steve Macdonald has brought home from his travels abroad: Indian marquetry tables in the comfortable sitting-room; hardwood elephants on the mantelpiece. Even the beds are made with Indian pure cotton sheets. Family photographs are everywhere, including an impressive study of ancestor Long John Macdonald, the whisky distiller. Both Steve and Kate know the area well and will tell you all the local history, like the sad tale of the 'pressed' boys imprisoned in the dungeon of the laird's house and smuggled through a tunnel to the waiting boats for enforced service in the Navy.

Guests take their meals in the attractive quarry-tiled dining-room, where books of local interest and paintings by local artists are for sale. Outside is a patio bright with tubs of flowers and, beyond, a magnificent view of An Teallach, the highest mountain on the peninsula.

Dinner might start with broccoli-and-Stilton soup or local scallops cooked in garlic and herb butter, followed by stuffed pork fillet or (in summer) wild salmon with a dill or lemon sauce, and a pudding like fresh fruit pavlova or lemon syllabub. Nothing is frozen; and Kate can produce authentic Indian meals if desired. Morning coffee, lunch and afternoon tea are available during the season, and Kate's sheer enthusiasm in all she does is a delight.

OSPREY HOTEL
Kingussie, Inverness-shire, PH21 1EN (Highland)
Tel: 01540 661510

D M PT S X

Nearest main road: A9 from Inverness to Perth.

8 Bedrooms. £18–£20 (less for 6 nights). Some have own bath/shower/toilet. Tea/coffee facilities. Views of garden, village. No smoking (in some). Washing machine on request.
Dinner. £18.25 for 4 courses (with choices) and coffee at 7.30pm. Vegetarian or special diets if ordered. Wine can be ordered. No smoking. **Light suppers** if ordered.
2 Sitting-rooms. With central heating, TV. No smoking (in one). **Bar.**
Small garden.

It takes most guests a little while to realise what they're walking on when they enter this small, welcoming hotel in the little town of Kingussie; for others the pattern on the carpet beneath their feet resolves itself almost immediately into . . . ospreys, specially commissioned for the hotel by a previous owner. The sofas and chairs in the cosy television room, and the tartan drapes in the dining-room, echo the red and green of the osprey carpet, while the bigger sitting-room across the hall has a bar offering some 20 malt whiskies to choose from. There is one bedroom on the ground floor, with shower-room; upstairs, cheerful colour schemes in which blue and green predominate make every bedroom a delight, though one with sweet-pea wallpaper is particularly attractive.

The Burrows came here in 1990, when Robert sought a change from the quarrying business he had been in for 30 years, and Aileen's job in a local government rating department was transformed at a stroke by the introduction of the poll tax. They took over a business whose reputation for good food was already long established, and Aileen has kept up the high standard, winning coveted accolades for her cooking. The dinner menu, which changes daily, always offers a choice of meat, fish and vegetarian dishes, with several options of starter and pudding. Typically, you might be offered cream of pea soup or avocado, cheese and grapefruit salad to start; Scotch sirloin steak with port-and-Stilton sauce; kiwi meringue, sticky toffee pudding, or a heady mixture of Drambuie or whisky with fresh fruit, oatmeal, honey and cream; and cheeses. On the breakfast menu might be porridge with cream, stewed prunes, home-made yogurt, haggis, oak-smoked haddock and oatcakes. Bread and marmalade are home-made; eggs free-range.

Kingussie is now bypassed by the A9, but remains within easy reach of Aviemore and the Cairngorms. It has its own Highland Folk Museum, and you can watch sheepdogs at work at Leault Farm near Kincraig.

PARAMOUNT
Main Street, Town Yetholm, Roxburghshire, TD5 8RF (Borders)
Tel: 01573 420505
South-east of Kelso. Nearest main road: A698 from Hawick to Coldstream.

3 Bedrooms. £19.50. All have own bath/shower/toilet. Tea/coffee facilities. TV. Views of town, country. Washing machine on request.
Dinner. £12 for 3 courses and coffee at 6.30pm or times to suit guests. Non-residents not admitted. Vegetarian or special diets if ordered. Wine can be brought in. **Light suppers** if ordered.
1 Sitting-room. With open fire, central heating, piano, record-player. Bar.
Small garden.

Possibly the only house in Scotland named after a favourite ram, Paramount is a charming mid-terrace guest-house facing the green in the conservation village of Town Yetholm (not to be confused with Kirk Yetholm, half a mile away, where the 270-mile Pennine Way ends). No one knows how old the original one-storey building is; the first floor was added in 1875, and the name was supplied by the carpenter who converted the house to its present immaculate standard, who had once been a shepherd.

Bedrooms are light and pretty, with white walls, white-and-gold furniture and creamy curtains, and in one, which has a lovely view of Stearough Hill, coronet drapes over the beds. Meals are taken in the attractive sitting/dining-room downstairs, fresh with cane and pine and William Morris fabrics; and there is a sitting-area upstairs too.

Marilyn MacKenzie serves such dinners as home-made mushroom soup or fish pâté, chicken provençal or trout (hot or cold), and meringues or lemon cheesecake.

Town Yetholm, like many border towns, still follows the ancient custom of 'common riding', originally instituted to remind the inhabitants of their territorial rights and privileges, and to warn potential intruders to keep their distance. The event takes place each June, and attracts many visitors to an area which at all times has much to offer. Robert Burns visited nearby Jedburgh in 1787 and spoke of its 'charming, romantic situation'; an earlier visitor was Mary Queen of Scots, who arrived in October 1566 to hold a circuit court and nearly died here after collapsing on her return from a 50-mile ride to visit the Earl of Bothwell, lying wounded at Hermitage Castle in Liddesdale.

Earlier visitors still were the monks who made the pilgrimage to Jedburgh Abbey; the so-called 'Capon tree' (from 'Capuchin') just south of the town is the last survivor of ancient Jedburgh Forest, through which they used to travel, perhaps resting under this very tree.

PITMURTHLY FARM
Redgorton, Perth, PH1 3HX (Tayside)   Tel: 01738 828363
North of Perth. Nearest main road: A9 from Perth to Inverness.

3 Bedrooms. £15–£18 (less for 6 nights). One has own bath/shower/toilet. Tea/coffee facilities. TV (in one). Views of garden, country. Washing machine on request.
Light suppers by arrangement.
1 Sitting-room. With open fire, central heating, TV.
Large garden.

The prefix 'Pit' in Scottish place-names – like Pitlochry – shows that the name is Pictish. The Picts lived north of the Forth in the first centuries AD, until in the year 843 Picts and Scots (from Ireland) were united under one king and the word fell out of use.

There has been a dwelling at Pitmurthly since Pictish times. The present 19th-century house sits over a cellar (with well) of much greater antiquity, and it is possible this could have been the site of a Pictish castle. Still, no echo of bloodier times need trouble today's visitor to Christine and Rob Smith's pleasantly furnished house, though Christine is fascinated by the history of the place and needs little encouragement to talk about it. Two romantic victims of the Plague lie buried at nearby Almondbank; a more recent celebrity to have stayed at Pitmurthly was Jan Struther, creator of Mrs Miniver, who married into a local family.

A blazing fire welcomes you into the sitting-room, furnished with lots of comfortable chairs, antiques and family photographs; bedrooms are simply decorated, with delicately patterned fabrics and lovely views. There is a huge downstairs bathroom, and a fine set of Victorian dining-chairs in the dining-room, where guests breakfast off blue-and-white china. Porridge, fresh fruit, herring in oatmeal and kippers might be on offer. Christine serves light suppers only, but recommends a selection of good nearby restaurants, especially the Almondbank Inn, a couple of miles away.

Pitmurthly is a working farm, where Rob (who was born here) fattens cattle and grows malting barley and Record potatoes (you might find yourself taking a few of the latter home). Visitors are welcome to look round the farm.

This quiet valley, just off the A9 and five minutes from Perth, is an excellent base from which to tour eastern and central Scotland.

Readers' comments: Extremely comfortable and welcoming, lovely breakfasts, a charming hostess.

PORTINNISHERRICH FARM C D
by Dalmally, Argyll, PA33 1BW (Strathclyde)   Tel: 018664 202
West of Inveraray. Nearest main roads: A816 from Lochgilphead to Oban and A819 from Inveraray to Dalmally.

rear view

2 Bedrooms. £17.50 (less for 8 nights). Both have own bath/shower/toilet. Tea/coffee facilities. Views of garden, country, loch. No smoking.
Dinner. £12.50 for 3 courses and coffee at times to suit guests. Non-residents not admitted. Vegetarian or special diets if ordered. Wine can be brought in. No smoking. **Light suppers** if ordered.
1 Sitting-room. With wood-burning stove, central heating, TV. No smoking.
Large garden.
Closed from October to March.

There used to be a ferry from Portinnisherrich – to 'New York'! The ferry no longer exists, but there is still a landing-place on the opposite shore which was used in the 17th century by a charcoal-burning company based in York as the shortest route between Oban and Inveraray. In those days Portinnisherrich was a waterside inn, possibly patronised a century later by Boswell and Johnson when they passed this way on their travels.

Today, Richard and Pat McKenzie welcome bed-and-breakfast guests again to their 80-acre farm on the shore of Loch Awe, the longest freshwater loch in Scotland (for statistics-seekers, Loch Lomond has the largest surface area and Loch Ness the greatest volume, while Loch Morar is the deepest lake in Europe). The biggest wild brown trout ever caught by rod in Britain was lifted from the loch in 1992. Boats are available for fishing, or just for excursions on the loch, for instance to Innischonnel, 14th-century seat of the earls of Argyll, a mile up the shore.

Pat uses local produce as much as possible in the kitchen: the farm's own lamb, for example, or fish (salmon, trout, pike) from the loch, or venison; smoked salmon or venison might appear as a starter, with crème Margot (with caramel mixed in) for pudding.

A magnificent Jacobean chest dominates the dining-room, whose walls are hung with flower paintings and a batik done by friends of the McKenzies; in the cosy sitting-room – part of the original house – is a signed lithograph of one of David Shepherd's paintings of big cats. The bedrooms are light and airy, with pale carpets and pine beds; in one, the fabrics are pretty with butterflies and vetch, while boldly patterned curtains complement cream bedcovers in the other.

The house, with its mile and a half of private shore, is beautifully situated midway between two main routes to Oban; there are ancient stone cairns in the forest behind it, and a ruined chapel nearly 1000 years old on an island in front.

PURGAVIE FARM
Lintrathen, Angus, DD8 5HZ (Tayside)
Tel: 01575 560213 (messages: 0860 392794)
West of Kirriemuir. Nearest main road: A926 from Blairgowrie to Forfar.

3 Bedrooms. £14.50–£15.50. All have own bath/shower/toilet. Tea/coffee facilities. TV. Views of garden, country. No smoking. Washing machine on request.
Dinner. £9 for 3 courses and coffee at times to suit guests. Non-residents not admitted. Vegetarian or special diets if ordered. Wine can be brought in. No smoking. **Light suppers** if ordered.
1 Sitting-room. With open fire, central heating, TV, record-player. No smoking.
Large garden.

David Clark's grandfather came to Purgavie ('place of danger') at the foot of Glen Isla in 1902; the family has farmed here ever since, with potatoes and barley now the main crops, while cattle and sheep graze on the hill. The large, comfortable bedrooms have flowery fabrics and wallpaper and lovely views over the glen; the dining-room is graced by a magnificent sideboard topped with a scale model of a World War I biplane made by Moira's grandfather.

With notice, breakfast can include smoked haddock, haggis or porridge. For dinner you may be offered lentil-and-vegetable soup; a casserole of local beef; and – an unexpected but addictive combination – home-made raspberry ice cream with dark melted chocolate: delicious. On another night you might sample 'clootie dumpling', a pudding of suet and dried fruits boiled in a cloth. After such a meal it is a pleasure to stroll down the deserted road, vivid with harebells and rosebay willow-herb, to the tiny village of Lintrathen, seeing the fishing boats silhouetted by the setting sun as it sinks behind the hills beyond.

Glen Isla is the most westerly of the lovely Glens of Angus. The 'Gateway to the Glens' is Kirriemuir, a small town best known as the childhood home of J. M. Barrie, creator of Peter Pan, although it has many other attractions as well. Barrie's birthplace is now owned by the National Trust for Scotland; the cricket pavilion on Kirriemuir Hill was given to the people of the town by Barrie himself. It now houses a 'camera obscura', one of the three remaining in Scotland, which uses optics and a mirror to provide panoramic views over Strathmore and the glens to peaks some 80 miles distant. There is an RSPB reserve at Loch of Kinnordy.

A few miles south of Kirriemuir is historic Glamis Castle, where the Queen Mother lived as a child and Princess Margaret was born.

148 QUEEN'S DRIVE
Glasgow, G42 8QN Tel: 0141-423 3143
Nearest main road: A77 from Glasgow to Kilmarnock (and M8, junctions 20 and 21).

2 Bedrooms. £16–£18. Tea/coffee facilities.
Light suppers if ordered.
1 Sitting-room. With central heating, TV, piano, record-player.
Closed from November to February.

When Glasgow hosted the now sadly defunct Garden Festival in 1988, the city suddenly had to find accommodation for unprecedented numbers of tourists – and quickly. Local newspaper campaigns fuelled the search for residents willing to provide bed-and-breakfast for visitors, and Beth Easton, along with scores of others, responded to the call. Slightly to her surprise, both she and the people who stayed in her huge Victorian apartment thoroughly enjoyed the experience, and Beth continues to offer a quiet, generous welcome to bed-and-breakfast guests. She does not serve dinner: there are Indian, Chinese, Greek and Italian restaurants just around the corner.

The flat is on the first floor of an imposing 1870s terrace in the south of the city – only a mile or so from Pollok Park and the Burrell Collection – and reached via a wide, curving, shallow-stepped stone staircase with wrought-iron banister. Inside, ceilings are high and rooms graciously proportioned; one bedroom has poppy-printed curtains, the other a cinnamon-and-peach colour scheme. Both are at the back, eliminating possible traffic noise.

The sitting-room – where visitors sometimes dance to Beth's collection of Scottish records, or play the baby grand piano – looks out over Queen's Park; and Beth, an admirer of Mary Stuart, will tell you how, in May 1568, the Queen of Scots sat her horse at the top of the hill you can see from the window and watched as her followers were defeated by the forces of her Protestant half-brother, the Earl of Moray. Indeed, she is said at one point to have ridden down among her men to rally them, and if necessary lead them in the charge herself, but she failed to inspire them, and the battle – her last – was lost.

It was a fatal turning-point. Aware that the tide of support had turned against her, rejecting the idea of flight to friendly France, Mary chose instead to throw herself on the mercy of her father's cousin, Elizabeth of England. She never saw Scotland again.

RHIAN COTTAGE
Tongue, Sutherland, IV27 4XJ (Highland)   Tel: 0184755 257
Nearest main road: A836 from Lairg to Thurso.

4 Bedrooms. £15–£16 (less for 4 nights). Prices go up in June. All have own bath/shower/toilet. Tea/coffee facilities. Views of garden, country, sea, river. No smoking. Washing machine on request.
Dinner. £10 for 3 courses (with some choices) and coffee at 7pm. Non-residents not admitted. Vegetarian or special diets if ordered. Wine can be brought in. **Light suppers** if ordered.
1 Sitting-room. With open fire, central heating, TV. Bar.
Large garden.

Stephanie Mackay's route to the northern Highlands has not been an obvious one: she has worked as a cowgirl in Australia and a shepherdess in Colorado, lived on a beach in Bali, been a hotel night-manager in New Zealand, and was Surrey County Council's first Gypsy Liaison Officer – her qualifications for that last post including a period spent teaching at the West Midlands Travellers' School, a charity which prepares travelling children for state school.

Now she is married to a Scottish fisherman, whose lobster and crab feature seasonally on the dinner menu, but it comes as no surprise to discover that besides her bed-and-breakfast Stephanie finds time to frame and market the paintings of a local artist whose studio is attached to the cottage, as well as sharing the work of the croft with Daniel – they keep sheep, pigs, ducks, hens and peacocks.

Rhian used to be the gamekeeper's cottage for the Loyal estate (Loch Loyal borders the road from Tongue to Altnaharra, with the peak of Ben Loyal to the west). Bedrooms are bright with cottagey fabrics and glorious views; most guests particularly admire the 'honeymoon suite': a beamy double room with its own shower-room in a converted byre across the yard. Breakfast options include herring in oatmeal, kippers, smoked haddock, black pudding, tattie (potato) scones, and home-made marmalade and raspberry jam; for dinner local produce is used whenever possible, including lamb, venison, beef and salmon as well as that lobster and crab when available. Soups are home-made, and puddings sinful!

This far northern coast of Scotland is spectacular, with glorious sandy beaches and magnificent coastal scenery to seaward, and the splendour of the Highlands inland. Roads are few and single-track; the rewards are worth the journey.

ROSLIN COTTAGE C D PT
Lagrannoch, Callander, Perthshire, FK17 8LE (Central)
Tel: 01877 330638
North-west of Stirling. On A84 from Stirling to Lochearnhead.

4 Bedrooms. £14–£18 (less for 7 nights). Tea/coffee facilities. Views of garden, country. No smoking.
Dinner. £12 for 4 courses (with some choices) and coffee at 6.30pm. Non-residents not admitted. Vegetarian or special diets if ordered. Wine can be brought in. No smoking.
1 Sitting-room. With open fire, central heating, TV, record-player.
Garden.

Although not strictly off the beaten track, Roslin Cottage has two back bedrooms (one on the ground floor) overlooking the garden and the fields beyond; even at the front, traffic noise is unlikely to be a problem after the evening rush-hour, quite minor compared with its counterparts down south. The house and its sister cottage next door – now the Myrtle Inn, which serves excellent meals – were built around 1707 for foremen on the local laird's estate. Linda and Alistair Ferguson came here in 1983 from Bedfordshire, where Linda taught middle-school French; Alistair – whose parents came from Perthshire – still teaches the deaf.

None of the bedrooms is large, but all are neat and comfortably furnished: flowery fabrics in one front room, tartan in the other, while foxgloves, honeysuckle and convolvulus twine over the bedcover in the upstairs back room. Guests share a very pretty green bathroom with a board-and-latch door and a riot of pot-plants.

The platter which is brought round at breakfast fairly groans under the weight of goodies on offer: Lorne sausage, fruit pudding, black pudding, haggis and tattie (potato) scones besides bacon and eggs; or lighter options are available if you wish. Dinner might be a soup of home-grown landcress, roast venison or lamb, and summer pudding.

Callander is ideally situated for visits to some of the loveliest parts of Scotland: Loch Katrine and the Trossachs are close (you can get there on the local bus, the Trossachs Trundler); Loch Tay and Breadalbane ('the uplands of Alban') within easy reach. There are castles at Doune and Dollar, Inchmahome Priory on the Lake of Menteith, a safari park at Blair Drummond. The tower of Dunblane Cathedral dates from the 11th century, the nave from the 13th; of the cathedral Ruskin said 'I know not anything so perfect in its simplicity, and so beautiful'.

THE ROSSAN C D M PT S X
Auchencairn, Castle Douglas, Kirkcudbrightshire, DG7 1QR
(Dumfries & Galloway) Tel: 01556 640269
East of Kirkcudbright. Nearest main road: A711 from Dumfries to Kirkcudbright.

3 Bedrooms. £12. Tea/coffee facilities. Views of garden, country, sea. No smoking. Washing machine on request.
Dinner. £8 for 4 courses and coffee at 7pm or times to suit guests. Non-residents not admitted. Vegetarian or special diets if ordered. Wine can be brought in. No smoking. **Light suppers** if ordered.
Large garden.
Closed in January.

Elizabeth Bardsley and her husband bought The Rossan with retirement in mind: considering that, as well as running the guest-house, she teaches the piano and re-canes and re-rushes chairs, retirement seems a distant prospect. But this is not all – Mrs Bardsley's forte is special diets. A coeliac and a vegetarian herself, she finds no difficulty in providing meals which are high or low in fat or in fibre, diabetic, wholefood, vegan, or any combination – though once a vegan who could not eat fat or gluten was a bit of a problem when the other four visitors each had different needs.

Meat-eaters stay here as well, being offered local steak, salmon, trout, or venison according to season. It almost goes without saying that fruit and vegetables, whether home-grown or bought, are organic, eggs from the Bardsleys' hens are free-range, and the home-baked bread is wholemeal. Though, clearly, there is no such thing here as a typical dinner, soup, stuffed tomatoes, and home-made ice cream might appear.

This is not a place for those who expect their hostess to be house-proud above all. But if you want to stay with caring and interesting people, The Rossan is for you, especially if you find an abundance of books and pictures more congenial than doilies and ornaments.

There is no sitting-room, though guests can linger at the table if they wish, as the bedrooms – each with home-made patchwork quilts – are meant to serve as bedsitters. Views are of the acre of garden or Auchencairn Bay and the Cumbrian hills.

Apart from people with dietary needs, birdwatchers come to The Rossan, especially for the sake of the several species of goose which overwinter in the bay. This is also a great area for fortifications – Celtic, Roman, mediaeval.

ST ALBANS

C(11) D PT S

Clouds, Duns, Berwickshire, TD11 3BB (Borders)
Tel: 01361 883285 (messages: 01361 883425 or 018907 61623)
West of Berwick-upon-Tweed (Northumberland). Nearest main road: A6105 from Greenlaw to Berwick-upon-Tweed.

rear view

3 Bedrooms. £13.50–£17 (less for 2 nights at weekends or 4 mid-week). Prices go up in May. Bargain breaks. One has own bath/toilet. Tea/coffee facilities. TV. Views of garden, country. No smoking (in two). Washing machine on request.
1 Sitting-room. With central heating, TV, record-player. No smoking.
Walled garden.

The romantic name of this byway in the town has nothing to do with the sky: once it was merely 'McLeod's' place.

The house, built about 1770, used to be a manse in the days when ministers lived in far greater style than now. The large sitting-room, for instance, has alcoves and deep-set windows; and the Kenworthys have furnished this and all rooms appropriately. Your breakfast-table will be laid with Wedgwood china and silver of the same period as the house. Breakfast may comprise something as hearty as kidneys, black pudding or herring in oatmeal if you wish; jams, and often bread, are home-made.

Bedroom no. 1 is of particular interest – not only because, Duns being so high up, you can see all the way to the Cheviot Hills (in England) from it but also because it has a chair that was the star of an Antiques Roadshow in 1992: it was made for the marriage of Gwen's ancestors three centuries ago, and carries the date 1676.

Duns, the county town of Berwickshire, used to be elsewhere but was so often burnt down by reivers (raiders) that it was re-sited on this hilltop for safety (the name means 'hill fort'). It gave its name to the Franciscan philosopher Duns Scotus, born here in the 13th century but buried in Cologne. His tomb carries the legend 'Scotland bore me, England adopted me, France taught me, Cologne holds me' to which, since 1993, might be added 'Rome beatified me'. (He affirmed the doctrine of the Immaculate Conception, and antagonists coined a new epithet, 'Duns man', which eventually turned into 'dunce'!)

Duns Castle, glimpsed from the house, is not open though its surrounding nature reserve and lakes can be visited – one rejoices in the name of Hen Poo; and Duns itself is an attractive little town. A stone on the hill close by commemorates the fact that the Civil Wars (in a way) started here, when Covenanters rebelled against the king in 1639. There is a Witches Hill, too, where Duns's last witch was burned in 1724.

SCANIA

M (continental breakfast only) **S**
Forres, Moray, IV36 0RE (Grampian)   Tel: 01309 672583
Nearest main road: A96 from Inverness to Aberdeen.

3 Bedrooms. £16–£18 (less for 4 nights or continental breakfast). Views of garden, country. No smoking. Washing machine on request.
Light suppers if ordered.
1 Sitting-room. With central heating, TV, piano. No smoking.
Large garden.
Closed from November to March.

Scania is an old name for southern Sweden, and Scandinavian overtones are evident in the design of this attractive 20-year-old house, home of architect Mike Shewan and his wife Norma, an artist and a hostess *par excellence.* A huge iron wood-burning stove in the hall provides much of the heating in the house; guests climb an open-tread spiral staircase to the kitchen/dining-room above, where breakfast might include oatmeal porridge, a compote of dried fruits with ginger and cinnamon, yogurt, and vegetarian options such as pumpernickel (black German bread) and cheeses. With your toast, choose from strawberry-and-elderflower or gooseberry-and-elderflower jam, both, like the marmalade, home-made. Light suppers only, but nearby Forres has a variety of eating-places; the Mosset Tavern is good.

Downstairs, two of the pretty bedrooms open off the guests' sitting-room – a comfortable area with a deep olive leather sofa, flowery curtains, striped wallpaper, and quantities of books. One bedroom has candy-striped wallpaper; the other roses stencilled round the head of the bed. A third bedroom, off the hall, is bright with mementoes of Norma's travels abroad; the shared bathroom, with pine-panelled bath, and a small kitchen where guests may make tea and coffee, complete the ground floor.

Outside, too, the Scandinavian feel is pronounced: Scania is surrounded by woodland, and conifers are plentiful. However, on closer inspection many of the trees turn out to be unfamiliar: fine specimens from the East planted by the owner of the Victorian mansion in whose grounds Scania was built. Owls and red squirrels live here, too.

Forres has won many awards in 'Britain in Bloom' competitions; it also boasts an excellent 18-hole golf course which is only half a mile from Scania.

SCHIEHALLION HOUSE D M
Glenshee Road, Braemar, Aberdeenshire, AB35 5YQ (Grampian)
Tel: 013397 41679
On A93 from Aberdeen to Perth.

11 Bedrooms. £14.50–£16.50 (less for 8 nights). Prices go up at Easter. Some have own shower/toilet. Tea/coffee facilities. Views of garden, country. No smoking. Washing machine on request.
Dinner. £10 for 3 courses (with choices) and coffee at 7pm. Vegetarian or special diets if ordered. Wine can be ordered. No smoking. **Light suppers** if ordered.
2 Sitting-rooms. With open fire, central heating, TV (in one). No smoking (in one). Bar.
Small garden.

Intriguingly named after a mountain in Perthshire many miles to the south-west, Schiehallion House is a traditional Highland lodge in a town whose royal connections go back long before Queen Victoria first visited Balmoral in 1848. In 1715, the Earl of Mar (nicknamed Bobbing John for his frequent changes of allegiance between Stuart and Hanover) raised the standard here for King James VIII. Unfortunately, the gold ball on the top of the standard pole fell off: an ill omen, the Highlanders considered, and indeed in little over two months the rebellion was crushed at Sheriffmuir.

Today Braemar is best known for its Highland Gathering, held on the first Saturday in September; there is also a Highland Heritage Centre, and the castle, 17th-century seat of the earls of Mar, where Hanoverian troops were garrisoned after the '45.

Alison and Neil Vaughan have created a guest-house of great charm and individual character. Blue and pink predominate in the bedrooms, which vary in size (there is a very pretty single room with flowery blue paper and fabrics); two have sloping ceilings, one with a lovely old inlaid bedhead, and rooms at the back have woodland views.

Meals, cooked by Neil, are excellent: dinner might start with game soup or haddock in cream-and-mushroom sauce, continue with trout or Scotch beef with mustard butter, and finish with clootie dumpling and custard (a Grampian version, with oatmeal) or Atholl Brose (whipped cream, toasted oatmeal, honey, ginger and whisky). Breakfast is the healthy variety: porridge, eggs poached or scrambled, bacon grilled. The blue dining-room, with its collection of blue-and-white plates and white jugs, is delightful; the sitting-room is warm and comfortable.

Nearby Ballater was a Victorian planned town: it started life as a railway terminus when Queen Victoria refused to allow trains to cross her land beyond, though now the track is for walkers only. There are nature reserves at Glen Muick and Muir of Dinnet, skiing at Glenshee.

9/B SCOTLAND STREET
Edinburgh, EH3 6PP   Tel: 0131-556 5080

4 Bedrooms. £16–£18. Tea/coffee facilities. Views of garden, city. Washing machine on request.
Light suppers if ordered.
1 Sitting-room. With open fire, central heating, TV.
Small garden.
Closed from November to February.

Anne McTavish lives in the city's so-called 'New Town', laid out in the late 18th century by James Craig (then only 22), its classical squares, crescents and symmetrical terraces of stone houses rivalling those of Bath. Along its south side runs one of Europe's most famous shopping avenues, Princes Street, overlooking valley gardens (the crag with Edinburgh Castle looms up on their other side) within which are sited the enormous 'gothick' monument to Sir Walter Scott (its designer was a mere village carpenter), the Royal Scottish Academy (in Doric temple style, with the young Queen Victoria seated on top), the Ionic National Gallery; and assorted statues and churches. Over the eastern end of the New Town looms rugged Calton Hill and its gardens which, being dominated by a partial replica of the Parthenon, has been likened to the Acropolis (and is, along with Edinburgh's cultural reputation, a reason why the city is nicknamed 'the Athens of the north'). The hill also houses the Burns monument, a circular Grecian temple; the Nelson monument, a vast, stone telescope; and other classical or 'gothick' buildings oddly juxtaposed. All this and more – including the Royal Museum of Scotland and the Scottish National Portrait Gallery – are within walking distance of Scotland Street.

Anne's duplex flat in one of the classical terraces retains such original features as shuttered windows in thick stone walls, panelled doors with handsome brass fittings, and a log fire in the sitting-room. Here the light effect of white sofas and yellow walls complements the paintings she collects and some of the interesting old furniture that is found throughout her rooms (she used to be an antiques dealer). One of her beds, a white iron four-poster, even has its original horsehair mattress, as firm as ever. Rooms are spacious, some with garden views framed by chinoiserie curtains. Anne has used big terracotta tiles on several floors, lined a large shower-room with polished marble, and herself stencilled leafy friezes on some of the walls.

Breakfast (with wholefood ingredients, fresh fruit and omelettes) is taken at a large oak table in her huge, beamed kitchen.

Unlike some proprietors, Anne does not raise her prices during the Edinburgh Festival which, every August, draws over 10,000 visitors from all over the world – but it is wise (here and at other houses) to book months ahead for this period.

THE SHEILING
Garve Road, Ullapool, Wester Ross, IV26 2SX (Highland)
Tel: 01854 612947
On A835 from Ullapool to Inverness.

7 Bedrooms. £18 (less for 6 nights). Price goes up at Easter. All have own bath/shower/toilet. Tea/coffee facilities. Views of garden, country, sea. No smoking. Washing machine on request.
1 Sitting-room. With open fire, central heating, TV. No smoking.
Small garden.

Exquisite studies of wildlife and Scottish landscapes by Ian MacGillivray cover the walls of The Sheiling; the artist's father used to be Duncan MacKenzie's boss. The paintings are renowned not only for their artistic merit but also for their technical accuracy, and limited edition prints are for sale.

Together with his wife Mhairi, a former nurse, Duncan now runs one of the most comfortable guest-houses in this book. It is appropriately named, for sheiling (sometimes spelt shieling) is a Lowland Scots word meaning 'shelter'. Duncan's grandfather bought the original house in 1934; in 1988 Duncan and Mhairi knocked it down and built the present one in its place. Much use of white paint, flowery fabrics, cane furniture and pine panelling ensures that all the bedrooms are extraordinarily attractive, but nos. 4 and 5 steal the advantage with views of Loch Broom. Three bedrooms are on the ground floor, and the carpentry throughout has been done by Duncan, whenever possible salvaging old oak rather than buying new wood. The sitting-room is big and welcoming, with comfortable Ercol furniture, a leather sofa, and well-stuffed armchairs.

The dining-room looks down over the loch, and you might be lucky enough to see seals as you breakfast on, say, oatmeal porridge with cream (heaven!) and home-made venison sausage flavoured with leeks, apples and Worcestershire sauce. Bed-and-breakfast only, but there are several good eating-places a short walk away in Ullapool (the Morefield Motel, for instance, serves excellent bar meals). A selection of menus is displayed in the sitting-room, and the MacKenzies will happily book your table. Free fly-fishing for brown trout can be arranged, too, and there are excellent laundry and drying facilities in the grounds, with a sauna, a rod-room, and secure garaging for motorbikes and bicycles.

Readers' comments: Very comfortable, most hospitable. A good genuine welcome – we have stayed on four occasions.

SKIARY   CDS
Loch Hourn, Inverness-shire, PH35 4HD (Highland)
West of Kinloch Hourn. Nearest main road: A87 from Kyle of Lochalsh to Invergarry.

3 Bedrooms. £43 **full board**. Views of country.
Dinner. 4 courses and coffee at times to suit guests. Non-residents not admitted. Vegetarian or special diets if ordered. Wine can be brought in.
1 Sitting-room. With open fire.
Large garden.
Closed from October to March.

Skiary is so blissfully remote that the house can only be reached by water or after an easy two-mile scramble along a rocky coastal path. Most guests are collected from the jetty at Kinloch Hourn, but if you choose to walk, leave your luggage in the car and John Everett will pick it up by boat – weather permitting. There is no telephone, and post is only delivered to Kinloch Hourn three times a week, so allow at least a fortnight for correspondence to confirm your booking and arrange a time for John to meet you.

The stone cottage, lined with wood throughout, has the rounded corners of a 19th-century turf-roofed blackhouse, where the family would have lived at one end and beasts at the other – an arrangement which persisted in this part of the world until well into the 20th century. The bedrooms, built into the roof, are reached by a steep staircase (best descended backwards) and lit by oil lamps (there's no electricity).

Downstairs, the bathroom has pine panels and a host of flourishing pot-plants, the white sitting-room a stone fireplace. Meals are taken in the kitchen, where dinner might be home-made soup (or mussels or mackerel if guests catch them!), a joint or a dish like chicken tarragon or steak-and-kidney pie, a pudding, cheese and grapes. Visitors stay on a full-board basis, with light or packed lunches, morning coffee and afternoon tea.

Boats are ready for guests' use, and John will take you on off-shore cruises in his 6-berth sloop – to Skye, for instance, or to Loch Nevis, where you can be dropped for a glorious hill walk back to the house. (Indeed, John's 'ferry service' means that there are ten Munros accessible from Skiary.) Cormorants, mergansers, eider, red- and black-throated and even the rare Great Northern diver have been spotted, as well as ringed plover, ravens and eagles; red deer, wild cats, badgers and pine martens too, as well as seals, porpoises, otters, and once a school of dolphins. This is Gavin Maxwell country: Sandaig, at the mouth of Loch Hourn, is the Camusfearna of *Ring of Bright Water*.

TAIGH DRUIMBEAG S
Drumbeg, by Lochinver, Sutherland, IV27 4NW (Highland)
Tel: 015713 209
Nearest main road: A894 from Scourie to Newton.

3 Bedrooms. £18.50–£20. All have own bath/shower/toilet. Tea/coffee facilities. Views of garden, country, loch. No smoking. Washing machine on request.
Dinner. £15 for 3 courses (with some choices) and coffee at 6.30pm. Non-residents not admitted. Vegetarian or special diets if ordered. Wine can be brought in. No smoking. **Light suppers** if ordered.
1 Sitting-room. With open fire, central heating, TV. No smoking.
Large garden.
Closed from December to February.

From the windows of two of the bedrooms of Taigh Druimbeag, you can still see the cottage where the Munro family lived at the turn of the century: father, mother, and seven children, including three sons who died in battle and a fourth who was killed in an accident. Mrs Munro's brother had emigrated to Canada where he made his fortune, rising to the rank of general in the Canadian army and eventually returning to Scotland a rich man. He offered to build his sister a new house, and she asked for one on the model of his own town residence in Edinburgh, which she much admired. The building was completed in 1907, and the two unmarried Munro daughters lived here until the 1970s. The house had been empty for ten years when Ron and Margaret Ward bought it from the sisters' Indonesian niece by marriage; the garden was a wilderness out of which they are gradually creating the most attractive order, and guests willing to offer appreciation, advice or manual labour are welcomed with open arms.

Indoors, painted floorboards are covered by a profusion of rugs and carpets, bedrooms are prettily papered with roses, and the sitting-room beckons with an assortment of comfortable chairs, a blazing fire, and two somnolent cats. All the furniture is solidly in keeping with its Edwardian surroundings: in fact the oak dining-table, chairs and sideboard were ordered through the shop in the village when the house was built, delivered to the beach by the 'west coast puffer' (one of the steamers which visited the Highlands and islands in the days when transportation overland was difficult), and brought up by horse and cart to the house, where they have stayed ever since.

Dinner might comprise soup or pâté, a roast with up to six vegetables, and one of Margaret's imaginatively sinful puddings: poached pears smothered in whipped cream and nuts; a delicious mixture of cream, whisky, honey and lemon juice on a digestive crumb base; or a confection of meringue, treacle and cream, to describe but three.

TARBET HOUSE   PT S
**Loch Lomond, Tarbet, by Arrochar, Dunbartonshire,
G83 7DE** (Strathclyde)   Tel: 013012 349
Off A82 from Glasgow to Inverness.

5 Bedrooms. £15–£25 (less for 2 nights). Bargain breaks. One has own bath/shower/toilet. Tea/coffee facilities. Views of garden, country, loch. Balcony (one). No smoking. Washing machine on request.
Dinner. £10.50 for 3 courses (with some choices) and coffee at 7.30pm or times to suit guests. Non-residents not admitted. Vegetarian or special diets if ordered. Wine can be brought in. No smoking. **Light suppers** if ordered.
1 Sitting-room. With central heating, TV, record-player. No smoking.
Large garden.
Closed from mid-October to December.

There are several Tarbets and Tarberts in Scotland. The name derives from the Gaelic word *tairbeart* meaning isthmus, and signifies a narrow stretch of land between two lochs where boats could be carried or dragged from one to the other. In this case, King Haakon of Norway is said to have dragged his ships here from Arrochar on the shore of Loch Long in the course of his pillaging expedition of 1263.

Seven hundred years later, the owner of the Tarbet Hotel built himself a practical, comfortable home on an elevated site high above the road running down the west side of Loch Lomond. Chris and John Harvey bought the house in 1990, when John took early retirement from the University of East Anglia (he lectured in environmental sciences); now he and Chris indulge their passion for hill walking and sailing by running holiday activities from Tarbet House, and have compiled a directory of walks starting from railway stations on the West Highland Line. They induct visitors into the mysteries of orienteering via a small introductory course in the garden!

Violent activity is not compulsory, however, and guests of a more restful turn of mind (or body) can relax in the open-plan sitting/dining-room, with slate fireplace and wood floor scattered with handsome rugs, and look out through huge plate-glass doors over the steeply banked garden (with tennis court) to the loch. Views from the bedrooms are even more spectacular. Lots of wood, white paint and pretty fabrics enhance the impression of light and space.

Dinner is not served every night (Chris, like John, is an Open University tutor, and other commitments sometimes intervene), but when available might comprise cockaleekie soup or fresh peaches in curry mayonnaise, poached Scottish salmon or braised venison, and bramble-and-cinnamon cobbler or fresh fruit salad. Oatcakes appear at breakfast, and – if you're lucky – Loch Fyne kippers.

TAWNY CROFT   C(12) X
Isle Ornsay, Isle of Skye, IV43 8QS   Tel: 01471 833325
Nearest main road: A851 from Broadford to Armadale.

2 Bedrooms. £30–£32 **including dinner**. Prices go up at Easter. Both have own bath/shower/toilet. Tea/coffee facilities. Views of country, sea, burn. No smoking. Washing machine on request.
Dinner. 3 courses and coffee at 7.30pm or other times by arrangement. Non-residents not admitted. Vegetarian or special diets if ordered. Wine can be brought in. No smoking. **Light suppers** if ordered.
1 Sitting-room. With wood-burning stove, central heating, TV. No smoking.
Garden.

Pictures of wildlife hang everywhere in this converted 1880 croft house: not only Pat Cottis's own cross-stitch representations of interesting plants, but also original watercolours and limited-edition prints by Eileen Soper, a founder member of the Society of Wildlife Artists. Lovely wooden objects turned by Roger's father are also in use or on display: beautifully carved fruits and an hourglass in the dining-room; clocks in the bedrooms.

The white-painted dining-room was the original croft house, now warmly lined with wood and elegant with blue velvet curtains, Ercol furniture, and Pat's cross-stitched place-mats on the dining-table. More Ercol graces the sitting-room, where big windows, cream curtains and white walls contribute to the impression of light and space, despite the comfortable welter of books and pictures. Doors at one end open into the conservatory, where a telescope has been set up to enable visitors to watch birds, look for otters, or just drink in the view.

Up the open-tread staircase, the bedrooms face each other along a short landing, the larger pink and white, with a dusky pink carpet and pastel fabrics; the other blue, with a clear view of the bat box in the wych elm outside the window.

Pat and Roger came here in 1992 from Staffordshire, where she worked in the NHS and he ran a design consultancy. They are keen natural historians, with a special interest in conservation and education, and will take guests on guided natural history walks to look for otters. They grow their own vegetables, which they serve with dishes like beef olives or pork chasseur. Pudding might be honey cheesecake or ginger crisp; the starter home-made vegetable soup.

Isle Ornsay – Norse for the island that can be reached at low tide – is famous for installing Skye's first public lavatory in 1820. And Gavin Maxwell, author of the otter books, lived in the lighthouse cottage.

THISTLE HOUSE
St Catherines, Argyll, PA25 8AZ (Strathclyde)
Tel: 01499 2209 (from April 01499 302209)
East of Inveraray. On A815 from Cairndow to Dunoon.

5 Bedrooms. £16.50–£18 (less for 3 nights). Prices go up in May. Four have own shower/toilet. Tea/coffee facilities. Views of garden, country, loch. No smoking. Washing machine on request.
Light suppers if ordered.
1 Sitting-room. With open fire, central heating, TV.
Large garden.
Closed from November to March.

There used to be a ferry between Inveraray and St Catherines; in those days the quickest way from Oban to Glasgow was via Loch Fyne and Loch Goil. So it was natural for an entrepreneurial Victorian ferryman to build an inn close to the shore at St Catherines, to cater for thirsty travellers temporarily stranded between Inveraray ferry and Lochgoilhead coach.

Coach and ferry are long gone, but Sandra and Donald Cameron still welcome guests to the former inn, now an exceedingly comfortable guest-house on the road running down the east side of Loch Fyne.

It is not only bedrooms at the front of the house which have fine views: the prospect – up the garden to the hills beyond – from the bay window in what used to be the library is just as attractive as that of the loch. Flowery fabrics and bright papers predominate; downstairs, the sitting-room and dining-room are decorated in shades of green. The curling-stones on the slate hearth belonged to Sandra's great-grandfather.

Light suppers only (make up for it with a Loch Fyne kipper for breakfast), but guests enjoy the nearby seafood restaurant (with oysters in season), or bar meals at the local pub.

Inveraray, sitting squarely across the loch from Thistle House, is famous for its 18th-century castle, seat of the dukes of Argyll and one of the earliest examples of the Gothic revival in Britain. The Jail is a 19th-century prison; and a three-masted yacht in the harbour houses a maritime museum. There are several gardens to visit in the area, like Younger Botanic Garden at Benmore, Crarae (rhododendrons) and Strone.

Prices are per person in a double room at the beginning of the year.

TIBERTICH FARM   S
Kilmartin, Argyll, PA31 8RQ (Strathclyde)   Tel: 01546 81281
North of Lochgilphead. Off A816 from Oban to Lochgilphead.

3 Bedrooms. £12.50–£16 (less for 4 nights). Views of garden, country. No smoking. Washing machine on request.
Dinner (by arrangement). £7 for 2 courses and coffee at times to suit guests. Non-residents not admitted. Vegetarian or special diets if ordered. Wine can be brought in. No smoking. **Light suppers** if ordered.
1 Sitting-room. With central heating, TV. No smoking.
Garden.
Closed from November to February.

Tibertich (pronounced Chibbish, meaning 'place of the well') is a working hill farm, where Chris and Barbara Caulton raise sheep and beef cattle in the lovely Kilmartin Glen. Chris, from Lincolnshire, used to farm in British Columbia, where he met Barbara.

    The stone farmhouse is at least a hundred years old, furnished with Canadian pine (darker than its British counterpart) and, upstairs, oak; pretty fabrics and arrangements of dried flowers. In the bathroom, a rambling ivy trailing from its pot on the windowsill echoes the leaf pattern on the green-and-white tiles.

    In former days, the shepherd here lived in one half of the house and the farmer in the other; now, meals are taken in the shepherd's half, a room comfortably furnished and decorated in yellow and blue, with a peaceful hill view. Here, Barbara serves such dinners as chicken supreme with three vegetables, a pudding, and cheeses.

    Outside, a former byre has been converted into unusually attractive self-catering accommodation, sometimes available to bed-and-breakfast guests looking for privacy and room to spread themselves.

    This part of Argyll is both beautiful and historic: there are Bronze Age burial cairns, stone circles and rock markings (Kilmartin Glen is thought to be the most concentrated site of prehistoric monuments in Scotland); an Iron Age hill fort, Dunadd, later capital of the 6th-century Scottish kingdom of Dalriada; and Carnasserie Castle, a mediaeval tower house.

    The west of Scotland is renowned for its gardens, of which the most famous is Inverewe; there are seven within an hour's drive of Kilmartin, including Arduaine (NTS), overlooking Loch Melfort, and Crarae on the shore of Loch Fyne, both with superb collections of rhododendrons and specimen trees.

TIGH NA MARA
Ardindrean, Wester Ross, IV23 2SE (Highland)
Tel: 01854 655282
South-east of Ullapool. Nearest main road: A835 from Ullapool to Inverness.

3 Bedrooms. £16–£20 (less for 4 nights mid-week). Prices go up in May. 5% discount on dinner, bed & breakfast to readers of this book staying two nights **or more** (except July, August and bank holiday weeks). One has own bath/toilet. Views of garden, country, sea loch. No smoking. Washing machine on request.
Dinner. £13.50 for 4 courses and coffee from 8pm. Vegetarian or special diets if oat-tolerant. Wine can be brought in. No smoking.
1 Sitting-room. With wood-burning stove, central heating, TV, keyboard, record-player. No smoking.
Small garden.
Closed in January (except New Year).

Tigh na Mara, 'the house by the sea', is just that: the high spring tide on Loch Broom rises to about three yards from the front door. Before the lochside road was built in the 1930s, this was the community shop, ideally situated to serve a population whose principal means of transport was by boat; even now it can only be reached by land after a 200-yard scramble down a steep and frequently muddy slope.

Guests are amply rewarded for their efforts, however: Tony and Shân Weston, refugees from London's media rat-race, have created one of Scotland's foremost gourmet vegetarian and vegan guest-houses, where you might dine on vegetarian haggis in a baked onion, followed by oyster mushrooms and almonds in a whisky and lime sauce on wild rice or seaweed rolypoly, blueberry syllabub, and your choice of over a dozen Scottish vegetarian cheeses, including a vegan cheese from the island of Bute. Breakfast, too, is a vegetarian gastronome's delight, with a choice of porridge or any of a dozen cereals followed by the full works: poached or scrambled eggs, organic baked beans, cheese on toast, mushrooms, tomato, potato cake, soya sausage and vegeburger. There are oatcakes, crumpets and toast to finish, along with a vast array of jams and honeys, soya yogurt and fresh fruit.

A spiral staircase rises from the comfortable sitting/dining-room to two light and airy bedrooms and a wood-panelled bathroom. A few steps from the front door is the converted boat-shed, now an idyllic 'honeymoon suite' where you can enjoy a spectacular vista of the loch from the bed, and even the huge corner tub in the bathroom above enjoys panoramic views. The former wood-store at the side of the house has been pressed into service as a guest kitchen, enabling the Westons to offer self-catering accommodation at low season.

Visitors are welcome to play Tony's flute, or clarinet, or guitar, and there are books and games indoors, or bicycles, rowing boats, kayaks and a windsurfer outside. The attractions of Ullapool are only 12 miles away.

TIGH'N EILEAN
Taybridge Drive, Aberfeldy, Perthshire, PH15 2BP (Tayside)
Tel: 01887 820109
Nearest main road: A827 from A9 to Killin.

3 Bedrooms. £17–£20 (less for 8 nights). Bargain breaks. All have own bath/shower/toilet. Tea/coffee facilities. Views of garden, country, river. No smoking. Washing machine on request.
Dinner. £9 for 3 courses and coffee at 7pm. Non-residents not admitted. Vegetarian or special diets if ordered. Wine can be brought in. No smoking.
Light suppers if ordered.
1 Sitting-room. With open fire, central heating, TV. No smoking.
Small garden.

In a quiet road on the edge of the little town of Aberfeldy lies this substantial Victorian semi-detached house, overlooking the River Tay and the island which gives it its name (Tigh'n Eilean means 'house of the island'). Fifty yards away, the Tay is still crossed by an 18th-century hump-backed bridge built by General Wade, who was sent to the Highlands in 1725 to confiscate Jacobite arms and left his mark in the great roads he constructed between Crieff and Inverness, and between the garrisons at Fort William, Fort Augustus and Fort George.

Elizabeth Bowman has an enviable eye for colour and style, as well as a talent for sewing: the generous curtains with their luxuriantly deep pelmets were made by her, dressing-tables are draped with matching fabrics, and wooden chairs are painted in toning pastel shades. All the bedrooms are attractive, but the 'Jacuzzi room' is a particular favourite: steps lead down from the blue bedroom into a carpeted bathroom almost as large, complete with huge white corner tub and comfortable sofa. (When the walls of this bedroom were stripped back to their original layer of paper, Elizabeth found that the Victorian borders were virtually the same as the Laura Ashley ones she planned to use herself.) There is a delightful single room in pink, with pine panelling, and two rooms have views of the river.

In the sitting-room, walls of delicate lilac frame a comfortable mixture of antique and modern furniture; the dining-room has a display of blue-and-white china and interesting wood-carvings. Dinner might start with pea-and-ham soup or thick lentil broth, followed by local salmon, trout, lamb or beef, with fresh vegetables in season. For pudding, you might be offered apple pie, fresh fruit salad, or a freshly cooked pancake with ice cream and maple syrup.

TOPPS FARM
Fintry Road, Denny, Stirlingshire, FK6 5JF (Central)
Tel: 01324 822471
West of Denny. Nearest main road: A872 from Stirling to Denny (and M80, junction 5).

8 Bedrooms. £18–£20 (less for 3 nights). **10% discount to readers of this book.** Bargain breaks. All have own bath/shower/toilet. Tea/coffee facilities. TV. Views of garden, country. No smoking. Washing machine on request.
Dinner. £12 for 4 courses (with choices) and coffee from 7.30pm. Vegetarian or special diets if ordered. Wine can be ordered. No smoking. **Light suppers** if ordered.
1 Sitting-room. With central heating. No smoking. **Bar.**
Large garden.

This part of the lush Carron Valley is a Site of Special Scientific Interest, and Jennifer Steel had to get special dispensation from the Scottish Office to pick the ransoms (wild garlic) she uses in her imaginative cooking to flavour such dishes as salmon en croûte or stuffed chicken. Alistair, too, is no slouch in the kitchen: his carrot-and-orange soup is second to none, and he has a set of 'sizzlers' to ensure his rib-eye steaks are served piping hot. Food is a priority at Topps Farm, and a four-course dinner might comprise grapefruit-and-orange cocktail sweetened with local honey; a soup of locally grown tomatoes; Drumnadrochit pie (spiced game topped with puff pastry); and Glenmorangie gâteau (soaked in 'the' whisky and water). The breakfast menu includes stoneground oatmeal porridge, fresh trout, haggis and kippers; and for the stoutest-hearted lunch too is available on Friday, Saturday and Sunday, when you might be offered marinaded Orkney herring, crêpes with crispy bacon and ratatouille, or pasta baskets filled with smoked-haddock-and-chive mousse and mushroom sauce.

It is perhaps fortunate, therefore, that the bedrooms are on the ground floor. All are prettily furnished with flowery fabrics, wood-panelled walls and cork-tiled bathrooms. Pictures abound, Jennifer's needlework mingling with paintings by other local artists, a fine family sampler, a rare tapestry of Saul at the court of King Herod, and a collection of old etchings. Jennifer's beloved Limoges plates are also on display. She is a passionate gardener too; outside, convex-bottomed curling-stones are everywhere, and look likely to become a permanent feature, since the last time the ice in the area was suitable for the outdoor game was in 1978.

Those guests not immobilised by the quality and quantity of the food find Topps Farm an excellent base from which to explore the Trossachs, or to visit Edinburgh, Glasgow and Stirling.

TORGUISH HOUSE
Daviot, Inverness, IV1 2XQ (Highland)   Tel: 01463 772208
South-east of Inverness. On A9 from Inverness to Perth.

8 Bedrooms. £11–£15. Some have own bath/shower/toilet. Tea/coffee facilities. TV. Views of garden, country. Washing machine on request.
Dinner. £9 for 3 courses and coffee at 6.30pm. Vegetarian or special diets if ordered. Wine can be brought in.
1 Sitting-room. With open fire, central heating, TV, piano, record-player.
Large garden.

The imposing staircase of this former manse (childhood home of novelist Alistair MacLean) is dominated by a huge picture of the opposing armies at Culloden, four miles away, under which the entire battle is described in three succinct lines. Composing such a summary used, apparently, to be a standard challenge for Scottish schoolchildren, as Marjorie Allan remembers.

She and Alister came here in 1986 from Broughty Ferry, where they had a newsagent's. Incredibly, they opened the house to guests while Alister was still running the business near Dundee, and for over six months he raced up and down the A9 between the two. Now all that energy and enthusiasm is concentrated on Torguish, and seems to infect his visitors too, since many people who stay here enjoy day-trips to distant Skye, or Orkney, or Fingal's Cave. A favourite drive is along single-track roads to lovely Loch Maree and Gairloch in the northwest, but there are many attractions somewhat nearer at hand, too: Lochindorb Castle, or the ancient burial chambers at Clava Cairns.

Bedrooms are furnished in a variety of styles; six have working shutters, and several have their original fireplaces. One on the ground floor is ideal for those who find stairs difficult, while two huge family rooms on the second floor mean that children or larger parties can enjoy privacy and space. Particularly attractive is one room decorated in shades of grey, with a lovely view down the Nairn Valley.

In the comfortable sitting-room, with its fireplace of stone quarried in Burghead and its Caithness marble hearth, guests are welcome to try their skill on the Allans' accordion. There is a distinctly Scottish flavour to the pictures on the walls, and a tapestry of 'The Monarch of the Glen', done by Marjorie, hangs in the big, airy dining-room, where she serves such dinners as home-made soup; salmon, venison or lamb; and fruit crumble or Eve's pudding (sponge with apples). Breakfast might include haggis, fried fruit pudding or Portsoy kippers.

Readers' comments: Good honest value in a nice house; large, honest breakfast; large, comfortable rooms. A great welcome from a great character; so helpful. Nothing too much trouble.

TORWOOD LODGE   C PT
High Cross Avenue, Melrose, Roxburghshire, TD6 9SU
(Borders)   Tel: 01896 822220
South-east of Galashiels. Nearest main road: A6091 from Newtown St Boswells to Galashiels.

3 Bedrooms. £19–£20 (less for 6 nights). All have own bath/shower/toilet. Tea/coffee facilities. TV. Views of garden, country, river. No smoking. Washing machine on request.
Light suppers if ordered.
1 Sitting-room. With central heating. No smoking.
Small garden.

In a quiet residential road on the outskirts of Melrose stands this substantial Victorian house, the home of Pauline and Michael Schofield, who moved here from north Yorkshire in the mid-1980s.

Bedrooms are delightful, with bathrooms papered to match flowery fabrics, Redouté roses on the walls, and a deep bay window in a room of pink and palest green. The two bedrooms at the back of the house look out over the River Tweed to the beautiful border countryside beyond; in the front room a particularly cheerful colour scheme makes up for any shortfall in the view. There is a comfortable sitting-room downstairs.

Bed-and-breakfast only, but Pauline can recommend a wide range of eating-places in Melrose: the Station Restaurant is good, and the Hoe Bridge at Gattonside, just across the river.

Only a few miles from two major routes from England – the A68 from the north-east and the A7 from the north-west – Melrose is an ideal stopover on the long drive north, but deserves more than a one-night stay. Besides its own abbey and Priorwood Gardens, there is Sir Walter Scott's Abbotsford House to visit in one direction, and his grave in Dryburgh Abbey in the other. For walkers, the Southern Upland Way passes within a couple of miles of Torwood Lodge on its journey from east coast to west; lovely border towns like Kelso (abbey, Floors Castle) and Jedburgh (abbey, Mary Queen of Scots House) are not far away. There are gardens and historic houses like Mellerstain (an Adam masterpiece) to visit, and magnificent countryside all around.

> Facts (prices, etc) at the top of entries are supplied by the proprietors themselves. While every effort is made to ensure that these are correct at the time of going to press, they may alter thereafter; please check when you book.

TOWNFOOT FARM
Roberton, Lanarkshire, ML12 6RS (Strathclyde)
Tel: 018995 655
South-west of Biggar. On A73 from Abington to Cumbernauld.

2 Bedrooms. £14 (less for 6 nights). Views of garden, country, river. No smoking. Washing machine on request.
Dinner. £6 for 3 courses and coffee at 6.30–7pm or times to suit guests. Non-residents not admitted. Vegetarian or special diets if ordered. Wine can be brought in. No smoking. **Light suppers** if ordered.
1 Sitting-room. With open fire, central heating, TV, record-player. Piano.
Small garden.

To a Scotsman in Idi Amin's Uganda the memory of the lovely Clyde Valley must have been a lifeline: Rennie Craig (his unusual forename was his grandmother's maiden surname) had sold agricultural machinery there for 11 years before deciding it was time to quit in 1972. Luckily he had Townfoot and Cathie to come home to, and they still work the 50-acre farm, raising barley and hay and grazing cattle.

The old part of the house began life in 1850 as two stone-built farm cottages. The Craigs added an extension in 1976; now bed-and-breakfast guests are accommodated in the original wing, where they share a sunny yellow bathroom and a wonderful view of Dungavel Hill; the Tinto Hills (Lanarkshire's highest) are just beyond. Both bedrooms are neat and pretty: in one, rose-pink velvet curtains and a fawn carpet; the other pink and grey.

From the dining-room (with piano and modern oak table) you can see the head waters of the River Clyde; for the very energetic, the walk to its source and back is a popular day's outing.

Cathie's dinners are homely and satisfying, with an emphasis on interesting puddings: you might have home-made soup to start, followed by lamb, beef or pork with fresh vegetables, and ending with Fairlop tart (made with golden syrup, butter and dried fruit). Porridge is always on offer for breakfast, with kippers or haggis if requested.

Ideally situated for a stopover en route from the north-west of England to Glasgow and Edinburgh, Townfoot is also an excellent base for touring the whole of southern Scotland. Many visitors go to Culzean Castle on the Ayrshire coast for the day, or up to Loch Lomond; walking, fishing and golf are available close at hand. For unusual gifts, visit Broughton Gallery, one of only three in Scotland selected by the Crafts Council for the high quality of the work exhibited.

TYNEFIELD   C(5) M
Dunbar, East Lothian, EH42 1XG (Lothian)   Tel: 01620 860464
Off A1 from Dunbar to Edinburgh.

Tea/coffee facilities. TV (in one). Views of garden. No smoking. Washing machine on request.
Dinner (by arrangement). £12 for 3 courses and coffee at times to suit guests. Non-residents not admitted. Vegetarian diets if ordered. Wine can be brought in.
Light suppers if ordered.
1 Sitting-room. With open fire, central heating, TV, piano.
3 Bedrooms. £16–£20. Prices go up in May. One has own bath/shower/toilet.
Large garden.
Closed in December and January.

If, visiting the Queen's palace of Holyroodhouse in Edinburgh, you have admired the lovely curtains there, the likelihood is that they were designed and made by Whytock & Reid. Tynefield is the home of David Reid, so it is no surprise to discover how beautifully decorated it is, and with many distinctive pieces of the family firm's furniture from the 19th century.

Tynefield's elegant façade dates from 1820 but the spacious structure behind it is older. It is in a peaceful setting, with footpaths from the garden to the John Muir Country Park and the Tyne estuary, frequented by seabirds. The garden (with grass tennis court) is so outstanding that it is opened to the public under Scotland's Garden Scheme: a particular feature is the decorative potager (flowers and vegetables together) in a former cattle court. Everything seems to flourish in this part of Scotland which gets more sun and less rain than most areas, where the air seems to sparkle and the summer evenings are long.

In the snug sitting-room, coral-walled, are an 18th-century fireplace carved with seashells, and deep-set shuttered windows. Many rooms have decoratively plastered ceilings, complemented by pretty wallpapers, and ornamental mouldings on the grey/white doors. The graceful crinoline staircase is so called because its banisters were reputedly shaped to accommodate the billowing skirts of the 18th century.

Some bedrooms have Whytock & Reid furniture, and garden views (including a glimpse of a *trompe l'oeil* dovecote). The big ground-floor one, which opens onto the garden, even has its own log stove and armchairs, as well as its own bathroom.

Judy Reid not only produces traditional dinners (roasts, game, etc.) but is an accomplished arranger of dried flowers grown in her garden – these are for sale. Fruit at breakfast and vegetables at dinner are usually home-grown, too.

UPPER WOODINCH D

Dalguise, Perthshire, PH8 0JU (Tayside)   Tel: 01350 727442
North-west of Dunkeld. Nearest main road: A9 from Edinburgh to Inverness.

2 Bedrooms. £17 (less for 2 nights; further reduction for 4 nights). Both have own bath/shower/toilet. Tea/coffee facilities. Views of garden, country. No smoking.
Dinner. £12 for 3 courses and coffee at times to suit guests. Vegetarian or special diets if ordered. Wine can be brought in.
Light suppers if ordered.
1 Sitting-room. With open fire, central heating. TV.
Large garden.
Closed in December.

Joy Maclean loves cooking and her guests love the results, many returning year after year to sample such delights as cream of carrot and ginger soup or smoked salmon ramekins filled with smoked trout mousse; pan-fried pork fillet with prunes and Armagnac or monkfish, scallops and prawns in a creamy lemon sauce with filo pastry; and apricot roulade, lemon soufflé or raspberry brûlée. Joy is Cordon Bleu trained, so every detail of presentation and accompaniment is perfect. Even breakfast is an event, with stewed fruit (plums, apricots or apples) or fresh raspberries and strawberries, depending on the season, and at least half a dozen choices of marmalade and home-made jams.

The house, built in 1993 high above the road in 25 acres of woodland (the view down through the trees to the plain below, like the breakfast fruit, varies with the season!), is the perfect setting for this culinary magnificence, since Joy's priority as she worked closely with the architect was the comfort of her prospective guests.

There are always fresh flowers and fruit in the bedrooms, which are furnished in Laura Ashley style; a smoky blue carpet, cream walls and flowered fabrics give the sitting-room a light and airy feel. In the sitting/dining-room, guests eat together round a gleaming gateleg table. French windows from both here and the separate sitting-room open onto a sheltered patio for the use of guests.

Beyond Dunkeld (once the ecclesiastical capital of Scotland) lies the Loch of the Lowes, where the Scottish Wildlife Trust visitor centre is open every day from April to September (see page xxv). Great crested grebes nest here, and with luck you might see ospreys.

Joy will organise salmon and trout fishing for you, or pony-trekking, or golf; and there are lots of lovely walks from the house. Northwards is Pitlochry, with Festival Theatre and Edradour distillery; Perth, with routes in all directions, is less than half an hour away.

WEST TEMPAR HOUSE CDS
Kinloch Rannoch, Perthshire, PH16 5QE (Tayside)
Tel: 01882 632338
Nearest main road: A9 from Perth to Inverness.

3 Bedrooms. £16 **to readers of this book only** or £33 **full board** (less for 4 nights). Prices for full board go up in May. All have own bath/toilet. Tea/coffee facilities. Views of garden, country, loch, river. Washing machine on request.
Dinner. 3 courses and coffee at 8pm. Non-residents not admitted. Wine and spirits can be brought in. No smoking.
Light suppers if ordered.
1 Sitting-room. With open fire, central heating, piano.
Large garden.
Closed from 15 February to 15 March.

If you look closely at the pine panelling which is such a feature of this Edwardian shooting-lodge, you will see irregularities in the dimensions of the panels. This is because, extravagantly, the shipping magnate who built it arranged to have it panelled not with American pitch-pine but with the indigenous Scots variety – a tree not noted for the convenient regularity of its growth.

West Tempar House has suffered a chequered history since then. During the Second World War, it sheltered first the nuns from an Edinburgh convent and later a school for Glaswegian evacuees. After the latter incursion, the hapless panelling had to be stripped of its scuffed and peeling paint – except in the present sitting-room, which had been the school's staff-room.

Janet Mineyko, a Cordon Bleu cook, serves such delicious meals as Rannoch-smoked venison with melon or avocado; chicken and broccoli with cream mayonnaise, or stuffed haunch of venison with mushrooms; and chocolate brandy cake or a chocolate-and-meringue gâteau. If game or fish is on the menu it is likely to have been shot or caught by Andrew, a keen sportsman who will take guests stalking if they wish. At breakfast, you might be offered honey in the comb as well as home-made marmalade with your toast.

Views from the bedrooms are breathtaking: even from one of the baths you can look out over Loch Dunalastair to Ben a'Chuallaich beyond. Schiehallion, Perthshire's highest Munro, lies to the south.

The house is full of lovely old furniture and family paintings; a portrait of Janet's great-great-great-grandmother hangs on the stairs. The Mineykos themselves are delightful, warm but ungushing, and full of esoteric snippets of information about the area.

Readers' comments: Excellent. We have stayed twice and are quite enchanted by it all; delicious regional home cooking; the ideal spot for a peaceful stay in the Highlands.

WESTER MONIACK FARM
Kirkhill, Inverness, IV5 7PQ (Highland)   Tel: 01463 831237
West of Inverness. Nearest main road: A862 from Inverness to Dingwall.

2 Bedrooms. £13–£14 (less for 8 nights). Tea/coffee facilities. Views of garden, country. No smoking. Washing machine on request.
Dinner. £7 for 3 courses and coffee at 6.30pm or times to suit guests. Non-residents not admitted. Vegetarian or special diets if ordered. Wine can be brought in. No smoking. **Light suppers** if ordered.
1 Sitting-room. With central heating, TV. No smoking.
Garden.

If you visit Wester Moniack in July or August, be careful to look both ways before venturing out of doors; for this is the time when young athletes hopeful of winning glory at their local Highland Games train here for the heavy events. A carelessly tossed caber, or wildly thrown Scots hammer, could add an unexpected dimension to your holiday!

The Munros' 19th-century farmhouse is ideally suited to Kay's stated aim of welcoming guests to a 'friendly family home'. The bedrooms are warm and neat; downstairs are an attractive bathroom, a comfortable green-painted sitting-room, and a dining-room with a chaise-longue and a splendid sideboard bearing Ally's collection of trophies for those heavy Highland Games events. Here Kay serves such meals as home-made soup or salmon mousse; turkey steaks in a creamy apple-and-tarragon sauce with fresh vegetables (some home-grown); raspberry meringue gâteau; and cheese.

The farm, which raises beef cattle, sheep and barley, lies next door to Moniack Castle, a seat of clan Fraser since 1580, whose stables and old laundry have been converted into a successful winery. The fermenting room, workrooms, cellar and bottling room are open to the public, and you can buy country wines, liqueurs and various preserves to take home.

Walkers come here for the beauty of the surrounding countryside – Glen Affric and Reelig Glen are particularly popular – while children love the Munros' pet Vietnamese pig, Sophie, and Rosana the rabbit. Since Inverness is so close (nine miles) access to other parts of the Highlands is unrestricted, but the nearby attractions of the Black Isle (the peninsula bounded by the firths of Beauly, Moray and Cromarty) should not be ignored. Cromarty (with courthouse museum and Hugh Miller's cottage) is the Highlands' best-preserved 18th-century town; there is a remarkable collection of Pictish carvings in Rosemarkie, a ruined mediaeval cathedral at Fortrose, and a country park with llamas, wallabys, and a 5000-year-old burial cairn.

WHISTLEBARE   C M
Milnathort, Kinross, KY13 7RP (Tayside)   Tel: 01577 864417
North-west of Kinross. Nearest main road: A91 from St Andrews to Stirling (and M90, junction 7).

rear view

2 Bedrooms. £18–£20. Both have own bath/shower/toilet. Tea/coffee facilities. Views of garden, country. No smoking. Washing machine on request.
Dinner. £8 for 3 courses and coffee at times to suit guests. Non-residents not admitted. Vegetarian or special diets if ordered. Wine can be brought in. **Light suppers** if ordered.
1 Sitting-room. With open fire, central heating, TV, record-player.
Large garden.

Despite its proximity to the motorway and routes to all points, Whistlebare feels satisfyingly remote where it nestles in the Ochils above Loch Leven and looks across to the Lomond Hills in the east (early risers can hope for spectacular sunrises), or down to the Cleish Hills in the south. The house probably started life as a distillery worker's cottage. The distillery has disappeared, and the cottage has changed out of all recognition.

The bedrooms – one on the ground floor – have glorious views to east and south, and the large bathrooms are particularly good. In the dining-room, a set of fine dining-chairs encircles the glowing mahogany table, while old sporting prints hang on the walls and muted Paisley curtains frame the prospect over the garden to the fields beyond. Here Jenny Clavering serves such meals as home-made soup, chicken or game, and lemon meringue or apple pie; or guests can dine in one of the many good eating-places down in Milnathort and Kinross.

The gardens of Kinross House are open to the public. Loch Leven will always be associated with Mary Queen of Scots, who was imprisoned by her enemies on an island in the loch for over ten months, before escaping in May 1568. Within a month, her followers had been finally defeated outside Glasgow, and she had made the fateful decision to place her life in Queen Elizabeth's hands.

Falkland Palace (NTS), too, has associations with Mary: it was rebuilt as a hunting-retreat by her father, James V, and one of the young queen's 'four Maries', Mary Beaton, was the granddaughter of its hereditary keeper.

Castle Campbell at Dollar is worth a visit, and there are splendid walks in all directions for those who wish to leave the car behind. But a note of caution: hang on to your hats. The cottage next door to Whistlebare was called Windy Walls . . .

WHITEHILL FARM C D S
Nenthorn, Roxburghshire, TD5 7RZ (Borders)
Tel: 01573 470203
North-west of Kelso. Nearest main road: A6089 from Kelso to Lauder.

4 Bedrooms. £16–£17. One has own bath/shower/toilet. Tea/coffee facilities. Views of garden, country. No smoking. Washing machine on request.
Dinner (by arrangement). £12 for 3 courses and coffee at 7.30pm. Non-residents not admitted. Wine can be brought in. **Light suppers** if ordered.
1 Sitting-room. With open fire, central heating, TV.
Garden.

The border countryside is some of the most beautiful in Scotland, and the views from this early Victorian farmhouse are glorious: to the Cheviots in the south; north and west to the Lammermuir and Pentland hills. Bedrooms are gracefully furnished, some with William Morris fabrics, and the ones which look towards the Cheviots get the full benefit of the sun. There are two single rooms, and a pine-panelled bathroom.

In the sitting-room, David Smith's passion for horses is reflected in the pictures on the walls and even the upholstery on the chairs, while Royal Copenhagen figures provide a clue to Betty's particular interest: she used to breed wire-haired dachshunds. The dining-room has a fine old dresser and oak gateleg table. Dinner is served by arrangement only, and might comprise soup or salmon mousse, a casserole or roast, and port-and-plum mousse or lemon pudding. Cheeses are all Scottish, and served with oatcakes. At breakfast, fish is a popular option.

Lovely Kelso is near, and Jedburgh only a little farther off; in the former, don't miss the unusual octagonal church, built in 1773 and recommended by John Wesley as the best shape for preaching.

In June, look out for the 'common riding', relic of a centuries-old tradition whereby townspeople of the borders rode their boundaries to warn off intruders. In Hawick, the common riding also celebrates the victory of the youth of the town, who captured a flag from the triumphant English after the Battle of Flodden (1514). To this day the burgh flag is a replica of that ancient trophy.

Scottish bank holidays are not always the same as English ones. Most diaries indicate both.

WHITEHOUSE
St Boswells, Roxburghshire, TD6 0ED (Borders)
Tel: 01573 460343
West of Kelso. Nearest main road: A68 from Darlington to Edinburgh.

3 Bedrooms. £15–£17 (less for 5 nights). Two have own bath/shower/toilet. Tea/coffee facilities. Views of garden, country. Washing machine on request.
Dinner. £10 for 3 courses and coffee at 7–8pm. Vegetarian or special diets if ordered. Wine can be brought in. **Light suppers** if ordered.
1 Sitting-room. With open fire, central heating, TV.
Large garden.

Once a dower house for a duchess of Sutherland, this handsome Victorian farmhouse is now the home of Angela and Roger Tyrer, who enjoy putting into practice here all they learned about pleasing guests when they ran a hotel. In the elegant sitting-room, a rich blue carpet complements deep red and cream upholstery and cream walls; in the dining-room, chairs and a sofa are grouped round the fireplace for visitors to relax in before dinner. Pitch-pine shutters and doors add warmth and colour, and there is a delightful Thelwell cloakroom.

Bedrooms are charming; one pink with a pale green carpet and furniture unusually decorated with painted paper panels, another with blue walls and lacy curtains. There are two pretty bathrooms, and views are of the Cheviots or the Peniel Heugh monument, built to commemorate the Battle of Waterloo (1815).

For dinner, Angela uses fresh local produce whenever possible, starting perhaps with pheasant mousse or an unusual soup, followed by salmon or roast lamb, and a pudding like coffee-and-mandarin gâteau or home-made sorbet. Afterwards, guests can wander down the farm track to the banks of the Tweed; fishing can be arranged with Roger, who also manages shoots in season.

The area is very popular with walkers (the Southern Upland Way runs a few miles away), and Dryburgh Abbey, Smailholm Tower and Mertoun Gardens are near. Slightly farther afield are some of the great houses with which the borders abound: 16th-century Thirlestane Castle at Lauder, for instance, built on the site of a 13th-century fort; and Traquair, the oldest inhabited house in Scotland, where you can visit workshops demonstrating silk-screen printing, wood-turning and pottery, or taste the home-brewed ale.

WILLOW COURT C D M PT
The Friars, Jedburgh, Roxburghshire, TD8 6BN (Borders)
Tel: 01835 863702
Nearest main road: A68 from Corbridge to Edinburgh.

4 Bedrooms. £14–£18 (less for 4 nights). All have own bath/shower/toilet. Tea/coffee facilities. TV. Views of garden, town. No smoking. Washing machine on request.
Dinner. £12 for 3 courses (with choices) and coffee at 6.30pm. Vegetarian or special diets if ordered. Wine can be ordered. No smoking. **Light suppers** if ordered.
2 Sitting-rooms. With open fire, central heating, TV. No smoking (in one). Bar.
Large garden.

Willow Court is a modern, professionally run guest-house which has won acclaim from the Taste of Scotland for the excellence of its catering, and no host could be more relaxed or easier to get on with than Jane McGovern, an archaeologist who takes in her stride unexpected arrivals in the middle of a toddler's birthday tea, and juggles visitors, children and obligations with astonishing grace and charm. The bedrooms, with their pretty garlanded fabrics, are delightful, and from the sitting-rooms the view over the little town of Jedburgh, spread out below, is as intriguing as any of unspoilt countryside. All rooms are on the ground floor except one, a spacious family room built into the roof.

The dinner menu is à la carte, and might include, as starters, grilled Jedburgh haggis with an orange and whisky sauce or dill-marinaded Orkney herring with a yogurt and grain mustard dip. Main courses could be venison simmered in red wine and juniper berries, or salmon steak pan-fried in butter and deglazed with dry cider, followed by raspberry and kiwi pavlova or hot lemon and sultana pastry. Almost all the fruit and vegetables used in the kitchen are grown in the two-acre garden by Michael, whose parallel interest – in race-horses – is testified by the many photographs of his hurdler, hunters and point-to-pointers which cover the walls.

Meals are served in the conservatory, where guests can again enjoy the panoramic view over Jedburgh. Although the house is situated in a quiet residential area, the market square is only five minutes' walk away, and the town offers much of interest to the inquiring visitor. A public garden has now opened on the site of a dig directed by Jane when she first came to Jedburgh, and all the abbey ruins are worth exploring. There is Mary Queen of Scots House to see, too, and the castle jail.

WOODHEAD FARM
Old Carlisle Road, Moffat, Dumfriesshire, DG10 9LU
(Dumfries & Galloway)   Tel: 01683 20225
Nearest main road: A708 from Moffat to Selkirk.

Tea/coffee facilities. TV. Views of garden, country, river. Washing machine on request.
Dinner. £12.50 for 4 courses (with some choices) and coffee at 7pm or times to suit guests. Non-residents not admitted. Vegetarian or special diets if ordered. Wine can be brought in. No smoking. **Light suppers** if ordered.
1 Sitting-room. With open fire, central heating. No smoking.
3 Bedrooms. £20–£24 (less for 4 nights). All have own bath/shower/toilet. **Large garden.**

Most conservatories feel like an extension of the house. At Woodhead Farm, the conservatory feels like an extension of the garden as you take breakfast amid a welter of flowering plants, exotic and familiar, and water flows musically over a 'rockery' in the corner. Through the plate-glass walls, inside merges imperceptibly with out: a mature garden and, beyond, the lovely Dumfriesshire countryside. There are cushioned seats of Victorian cast iron; garden tables are spread with white cloths to receive, perhaps, porridge or a compote of apricots, figs and prunes, and smoked haddock poached in milk.

Sylvia Jackson, a Londoner, has travelled a long way to reach this idyllic spot. She had lived in Canada, San Francisco, Los Angeles, the Isle of Wight and Yorkshire before arriving to run a hotel in Moffat in 1968. Ten years later she married Murray and came to help him on this 200-acre stock-rearing farm.

When Murray first came to Woodhead in 1958 the house had no electricity. Now its Georgian façade (the original house is much older) shields an interior of comfort, elegance and great charm which tempts guests to return again and again. One bedroom has ferny wallpaper and French-style furniture; the brown-and-cream colour scheme of another is complemented by its brown-carpeted bathroom – big enough to merit a sofa – with cork-tiled walls and mirrors everywhere. In the third, the watered silk effect of the grey-green paper is in perfect contrast to vivid anemone curtains and bedcovers.

In the wood-floored dining-room, Sylvia serves cream of marrow soup, say, or one of lentils, bacon, tomato and cream; followed by the farm's own lamb, or spicy meat loaf, or farmhouse chicken; bread pudding with whisky and cream or fresh fruit salad; and cheeses. Vegetables are always fresh – home-grown whenever possible – and herbs are from Sylvia's garden.

Woodhead Farm sits directly on the Southern Upland Way.

EXPLANATION OF CODE LETTERS

(These appear, where applicable, in alphabetical order after the names of houses)

C Suitable for families with children. Sometimes a minimum age is stipulated, in which case this is indicated by a numeral; thus **C**(5) means children over 5 years old are accepted. In most cases, houses that accept children offer reduced rates and special meals. They may provide cots, high chairs and even baby-sitting; or games and sports for older children. Please enquire when booking. And do not expect young children to be lodged free, as babies are. Many houses have playing-cards, board games, irons, hair-dryers, maps, gumboots, bicycles, and so forth – just ask. Families which pick establishments with plenty of games, swimming-pool, animals, etc., or that are near free museums, parks and walks, can save a lot on keeping youngsters entertained. (Readers wanting total quiet may wish to avoid houses coded **C**.)

D Dogs permitted. A charge is rarely made, but it is often a stipulation that you must ask before bringing one; the dog may have to sleep in your car, or be banned from public rooms.

M Suitable for those with mobility problems. Needs vary: whenever we have used the code letter **M**, this indicates that not only is there a ground-floor bedroom and bathroom, but these, and doorways, have sufficient width for a wheelchair, and steps are few. For precise details, ask when booking.

PT Accessible by public transport. It is not necessary to have a car in order to get off the beaten track when public transport is available; houses indicated by the code **PT** have a railway station or coach stop within a reasonable distance, from which you can walk or take a taxi (quite a number of hosts will even pick you up, free, in their own car). The symbol **PT** further indicates that there are also some buses for sightseeing, but these may be few. Ask when booking.

S Indicates those houses which charge single people no more, or only 10% more, than half the price of a double room (except, possibly, at peak periods).

X Visitors are accepted at Christmas, though Christmas meals are not necessarily provided. Some hotels and farms offer special Christmas holidays; but, unless otherwise indicated (by the code letter **X** at top of entry), those in this book will then be closed.

ORDER FOR ENGLAND AND WALES EDITION

Name_____

Address_____

_____

_____

_____

Please send me _____ copies of *Staying Off the Beaten Track in England and Wales.*

I enclose a cheque/PO for £_____ made payable to *Explore Britain.* Price per book is £9.99 including postage and packing. Overseas: £11.50 (for Europe, the Republic of Ireland, and surface mail to rest of world) or £13.50 (for air mail to all countries except Europe and the Republic of Ireland); payment in sterling only. A new edition of this book appears every November.

This form, together with a cheque/PO, should be sent to Explore Britain, Alston, Cumbria, CA9 3SL, from where further copies of the Scotland edition are available too.